EARLY VICTORIAN ARCHITECTURE
IN BRITAIN

Publisher's Note
The original edition of *Early Victorian Architecture in Britain*
was published in two volumes, one containing an extensive discussion
and appreciation of early Victorian architecture by Mr. Hitchcock,
and the other containing a list of the illustrations the author had
collected and the plates themselves. This single-volume paperback
edition includes the original Preface, Acknowledgments, and first
chapter of the original, as well as all the illustrations. In the List of
Illustrations and among the plates themselves there are divisions
referring to chapters of the original book that are not reproduced
in this paperback edition.

YALE HISTORICAL PUBLICATIONS

George Kubler, Editor
History of Art: 9
The publication of the first edition of this work was aided
by funds provided by the Yale Department of the History of Art
deriving from a bequest of Isabel Paul.

EARLY VICTORIAN

ARCHITECTURE

IN BRITAIN

(abridged)

by Henry-Russell Hitchcock

A DA CAPO PAPERBACK

Library of Congress Cataloging in Publication Data

Hitchcock, Henry Russell, 1903-
  Early Victorian architecture in Britain (abridged)

  (A Da Capo paperback)
  1. Architecture — Great Britain. 2. Architecture,
Victorian — Great Britain. I. Title.
NA967.H552 1976 720′.942   75-35908
ISBN 0-306-80036-5

ISBN: 0-306-80036-5
First Paperback Printing 1976

This Da Capo paperback edition of *Early Victorian Architecture in Britain*
contains all the plates from Volume II of the original edition published in
New Haven in 1954, along with the Preface, Acknowledgments, and Chapter I
from Volume I. It is reprinted with the permission of Yale University Press
and, for the British market, of The Architectural Press, Ltd.

Published by Da Capo Press, Inc.
A Subsidiary of Plenum Publishing Corporation
227 West 17th Street
New York, N.Y. 10011

FOR JOHN SUMMERSON DOROTHY STROUD FELLO ATKINSON

who have helped most

PREFACE

> *History, to be accurate, must be thick enough*
> *to include the various levels of taste, to explain,*
> *or at least to expound, survivals as well as*
> *innovations, for frequently it is the conflict*
> *between tradition and novelty which produces*
> *the total culture of a time.*
>
> GEORGE BOAS

A satisfactory definition of Victorian architecture—Early, High, or Late—is not easily achieved. Neither "Victorian" nor "architecture," taken alone, is a word whose meaning need be obscure. Yet the complexity of their combined connotations gives a phrase that is ambiguous and even paradoxical to modern ears. Did any part of the Victorian Age produce *architecture* worthy of the name? Are Victorian ideas about architecture of any interest today? Or were they but confused heresies best ignored in a later age?

As some such questions arise in the critical mind around the phrase "Victorian architecture," so the historical mind may ask equally taxing ones: What, for instance, is properly meant by Victorian as applied to 19th-century culture? The Age of Victoria was a chronological entity defined by the sixty-four-year reign of the Queen; but can the same sixty-four years be considered also to frame a true cultural unit? If so, is that unit British only, more broadly Anglo-Saxon, or has it a wider significance in the general picture of 19th-century culture?

Above all, is the Victorian Age best considered as a single period? Or does it consist of a succession of subperiods, each more sharply characterized individually than continuous with the others? "Don't be Early Victorian," warned the Late Victorians; but our century abbreviated the warning to "Don't be Victorian." Now a change is well under way. By assuming that much of what is properly Early Victorian is but a happy aftermath of the respected Georgian—or at worst a playful excursus after the rigid rule of taste of the previous century—a great deal of the production of the 1830's and 1840's has in the last decade or two been removed from the artistic *Index Expurgatorius*.

The complete story of Victorian architecture rather resembles one of those endless novels typical of the period, over complicated in plot and subplot and crowded with quaintly named characters. The protagonists, moreover, are often so highly individualized that they seem like caricatures, or even fictional inventions, if their work and their opinions are merely sketched in outline. To attempt an over-all coverage of Victorian architecture in one volume is therefore as difficult—perhaps as futile—as to give an abridged version of *David Copperfield* or *Vanity Fair*.

This book is concerned with building production in Britain in the second quarter of the 19th century, or more precisely with that of the score of years from just before 1837 to just after 1852. Aspects of the history of construction are included that most Early Victorians did not consider relevant to the development of architecture as an art. Various characteristic manifestations of the period, moreover, which have generally been found unsympathetic in the past half-century will neither be excluded nor merely ridiculed. Willful omissions and blanket denigrations have hitherto tended to produce a picture of Early Victorian architecture that only Late Victorians, in their natural reaction against the ways of their fathers, would have recognized as plausible. An intentionally sympathetic study of Early Victorian architecture may hope to redress the critical balance without seeming to propose a "Victorian Revival."

Historians increasingly offer us an 18th century almost as full of movement and variety in the arts as the 19th was to be. The Georgians were never averse to new ideas in art, provided those who proposed them paid lip service to established cultural proprieties. As critics of art, moreover, and as technical aestheticians, the Georgians were more profound and subtler than the Victorians who later rang such curious changes on their most valid conclusions. Theory grew bolder, if also more confused, in the early 1850's just as the Early Victorian period was coming to an end.

Evidences of a lively eclecticism in Georgian taste are not difficult to discern in the byplay of surface fads patronized by a ruling elite. Among professional architects there was an unresolved mixture of real respect for the past, both Classical and medieval, untrammeled by excessive archaeological pedantry, and of serious enthusiasm for various new materials: some, such as iron, destined to be of major consequence later on; others merely shoddy substitutes like papier maché. Plenty of scandalous jerry-building went on in Georgian times; and in the handling of materials, old and new, there was both a continuing tradition of solid craftsmanship, even in machine work, and the most shameless gimcrackery. Time has distorted the balance, however, by wiping out most of what was *too* ill built or ill made in the 18th century.

In the present century those who are not specialists readily receive from the extant architectural remains of the Hanoverian period a single favorable image. If the 20th-century historian of Georgian architecture is to correct this popular image he must be coldly analytical, even cynical, in his approach. In presenting the architecture that succeeded the Georgian, on the other hand, one is perforce a sort of devil's advocate. To make out a plausible case for the serious study of Early Victorian building production, moreover, a more or less synthetic treatment is requisite. Broad categories, most of them already well recognized, must be utilized to subsume under a few headings the major new currents. Such a sorting out of the vast production of the period can help to make those currents comprehensible; they can then be recognized as valid expressions of continuing human aspirations, not mere manifestations of a perverse tastelessness. What seemed to contemporaries, even more perhaps than to posterity, a chaos of conflicting doctrine was by no means devoid of a few principles of positive taste that were widely accepted even by leaders in opposed critical camps. In controversy, naturally, the differences of position were loudly stated; the agreements were more usually tacit.

The Victorians were highly articulate and their self-critical writing is only too readily accepted today at face value. Some historians of the 19th century have been content to offer pictures of Early Victorian architecture that are, in effect, inherited from the period itself rather than freshly reconstituted. Lined up still with one or another Victorian critical faction, such writers have continued to present that faction's limited program as absolutely valid while dismissing the general run of Early Victorian building as laggard, preparatory, or outright vicious. Just as most political historians show their sympathies to be Whig or Tory, Conservative or Liberal, many writers on 19th-century architecture go all out for the "Greeks" or the "Goths." A few maintain that everything worth while derived from the continuance (or the revival) of some aspect of academic Classical tradition. Rather more historians and critics have continued to propagate the ideas of the medievalizing party. Many, for instance, accept its avowed functional principles and reject its practice; earlier in the century there were some architects who seemed to do exactly the reverse (alas, a few are around still). The learned and the professional world at least is unable to ignore Early Victorian architecture any longer, even if there is little current agreement as to its true value and meaning.

On the whole the ordinary cultivated person's grasp of what is Victorian, and even of why certain buildings are Victorian, is better than his assumed understanding of what is Georgian. It bears some resemblance at least to concepts that have historical and cultural reality, more perhaps than do some of the subtle and conflicting interpretations historians have been offering. But whether what is recognized as Victorian be rejected or embraced by the casual observer—and the public's reaction seems to grow more favorable all the time, at least to work of the Early Victorian decades—this general

recognition remains highly uncritical. If we may judge from the faint manifestations of a Victorian "Revival" (fortunately almost entirely restricted to
the realm of fashion, furniture, and decoration) what is most recognizably
Victorian is the lowest vernacular of the age. Victorian leaders of taste,
whether designers or critics, would have rejected as deplorably Philistine
most of what now sells best in the antique shops.

Among those of more discrimination, a tentative distinction between Early
Victorian and Late is often made today; the former, in principle, is considerably more widely appreciated than the latter, by laymen if not by specialists. (High Victorian is still pretty much a critic's and historian's term).
But what is currently called "Early Victorian" may easily in fact be Late
Georgian, not only in date but quite characteristically in style also—or,
for that matter, it may be provincial work produced relatively late in the
century. Blanket approval of the artistic production of an age is as stupid
as is all-inclusive scorn. The wares of second-hand dealers turned merchants
of the "antique" reveal how little the rising favor of Victoriana has yet developed any relevant artistic criteria. The shops still cater chiefly to that
childish delight in the quaint with which the reassessment of the production of all periods of the past has begun.

Architecture is, properly speaking, not collectible. Certain preservation
programs amount to collecting buildings, however, and some museums col-
lect—perhaps unwisely—what are called "period rooms." In general the
more closely the attitudes and the activities of enthusiasts for the architecture of any period approach those of the collector, the more harm they do.
Yet the monuments of any period of the past require intelligent understanding and respect from posterity if they are not all to be destroyed outright or
else quite denatured by unsympathetic renovation.

The present state of general interest in Early Victorian architecture is
most unsatisfactory. The wrong things are too often selected for preservation merely because they conform to the public's naive idea of what is characteristic; the major monuments are either neglected or perhaps ruined by
tactless remodeling. The possibility of arriving at a well-balanced picture of
Victorian architecture is diminishing rapidly despite the tremendous volume
of Victorian production which still remains intact. With the irony that plagues
all preservation activities, the blanket refusal to consider any 19th-century
structures worth saving has begun to lift, at least for much work of the
1830's and 1840's, before there is sufficient knowledge of what should be
saved, and before proper techniques of maintenance and restoration without stylistic distortion have even been accepted as desirable.

The author aims to sort out the architectural remains of the Victorian
Age into their principal categories in order that relative aesthetic quality

and historical significance within those categories may become more recognizable. Such a sorting out must in the first place be chronological; therefore this book deals only with the late 1830's, the 1840's, and the early 1850's. But within that main chronological category there are typological and stylistic subcategories that require distinct recognition also.

Modern architectural theory often assumes that all types of edifice can (and even should), in any period, be designed in much the same way. The obvious readiness of the mid-19th century to utilize alternative stylistic forms in different fields, already deprecated by severe critics at the time, seems peculiarly reprehensible to us in a way it did not to the Late Victorians or even to most men of the early 20th century. But judgment should at least be suspended until Early Victorian production has been carefully examined. Even those mid-19th-century architects who were positive fanatics about "style" generally employed without shame a more or less extensive variety of modes when their practice included various different types of edifice. Other leaders of taste were quite frank in defense of a studied eclecticism, intentionally varied according to purpose and location. Different subcategories of type and of nominal "style," when broadly interpreted, therefore correspond to real subdivisions in Early Victorian production. They will also be found to be at least loosely interrelated; one type supposedly requiring one style and another, another, according to a tacitly accepted scheme of semi-functional symbolism.

Too strict a typological approach to Early Victorian building production tends to mask the relative unity of visual taste within the period. It also obscures the interchanges by which new architectural ideas, whether technical or visual, passed back and forth between groups of architects who specialized in different kinds of commissions. On the other hand, to take the supposed "battle of the styles," or even the actual confused free-for-all of stylistic factions, at face value is to ignore exactly the characteristics that are prime to the Early Victorian as a style-phase in its own right. Both the subcategories based on various building types and those based on what should be called "stylisms" or modes rather than "styles" must be kept elastic. The latter should be defined, as it were archaeologically, from the extant material rather than a priori, according to the pat terms of the period. Yet the contemporary terms, with their various favorable and unfavorable connotations, are themselves significant; for they provide a part of the data with which the historian must work in interpreting buildings of the period.

Certain individual Victorian architects, both Early and Late, have achieved fame out of proportion to their deserts, while others of as great significance have been totally forgotten. Accidents of contemporary publicity or even conscious campaigns, worthy of our own period of planned "public relations," explain some excessive reputations that now hardly need deflation. Then there are those men, often not conspicuously successful nor widely known at present, who have yet been widely accepted by later architects and critics as models of correct views and of conscientious devotion to their art—if not so often, in more absolute terms, as great masters of architectural design. It must be an important part of the historian's duty to seek out also the significant work of more obscure men with whom neither contemporaries nor posterity have been much concerned. And there are whole ranges of Early Victorian building production, ranges which the age largely ignored or consistently denigrated as architecture, which deserve total reassessment. The study of Victorian architecture need rarely be based on internal evidence only; most of what is of consequence can be linked by historical documentation with specific architects, engineers, or builders. Unfortunately, the examination of the total existing documentation must still proceed much further before all that ought to be known becomes readily accessible.

The disagreement, if one may so put it, between the scholars and the public on the subject of Early Victorian architecture is partly the fault of the former. Most writers have been excessively preoccupied with a few rather special edifices or with certain particular lines of development, ignoring too often the buildings with which the public is most familiar. Some of those special edifices were famous enough in their own day, like the Crystal Palace; others were hardly known outside a small inner circle of the aesthetic elite. Important as such things are, they cannot be considered to epitomize the whole Early Victorian period. No more can three or four of the more prominent urban edifices, such as the Houses of Parliament, the Reform Club, and St. George's Hall, when their images are projected on the screen in brief introductory lectures on the history of art, give any just idea of the general character of architectural production in the 30's, 40's, and early 50's.

Exceptional quality in Early Victorian building should be acclaimed wherever it may be found. The critical attitude that ignores all work without conscious artistic pretention and the opposing one which sees in architecture only more or less accomplished solutions of engineering problems are both forms of intellectual snobbery. It is therefore desirable to examine with equal care what the Early Victorians considered to be their most significant works and also those which our later age has accepted as worthy forerunners of its own architecture; they are often very different. The mass of ordinary buildings from which the public derives its understanding of Early Victorian architecture requires serious study too. That production was vast; nearly just is the estimate of those who have dismissed most of it as contemptible. Only a sampling technique, therefore, can hope to present its principal characteristics without tedious repetition and any analysis must perforce be almost more sociological than architectural.

Beyond the range of the better known architects who are mentioned in the existing histories, however, there are many modest individuals, men who never reached the metropolis or built a public monument, who are deserving of posterity's recognition for their personal achievement, or merely for their highly original ideas. Some anonymous buildings, moreover—anonymous at least thus far, in the absence of detailed local research—equal in quality the most conspicuous buildings by the most famous professional leaders. But even the work of those leaders who have already been the subject of individual biographies has rarely been illustrated thoroughly or with much discrimination. The lives and the opinions of such men are better documented than their buildings, with which this book is primarily concerned.

Northampton, Mass.
June 3, 1954

ACKNOWLEDGMENTS

During the ten years this book has been in active preparation there has accumulated a weight of obligation almost impossible to recall in full, much less to acknowledge in detail. Hazarding the accidental omission of some names, I must nevertheless attempt to set down here my thanks to all those who have been helpful and to express generic debts that are more precisely itemized in the separate entries of the List of Illustrations and, by implication at least, in various precise references to books and articles in the main text.

The three friends to whom this book is dedicated are those to whom my obligation is greatest. In 1945–46 John Summerson and Dorothy Stroud made me free of the Soane Museum, and in the comfort of their office serious work on this book began. Both of them, again and again, guided and accompanied me on expeditions through Victorian London and sustained me in all sorts of other ways. I am also using three photographs provided by Mr. Summerson; a plan from his *John Nash;* and much information, as well as short quotations, from his *Georgian London.* Over and above this, however, I know that a very large proportion of the 83 photographs in this book which come from the National Buildings Record were taken by him or for him during the war when he had the forethought to see that 19th-century as well as earlier architecture should be properly documented. Miss Stroud aided me in obtaining photographs from *Country Life,* of which ten are reproduced in this book with the permission of the proprietors. Fello Atkinson read most of my chapters and discussed them with me in detail. With him I have also visited many major monuments and never failed to see more through his eyes than I should have done with my own alone.

In the latest stages of the preparation of this book I owe a great deal to various friends at Yale: Lewis Perry Curtis, editor of the Yale Historical Publications, George Kubler, editor of the History of Art Publications, Sumner McKnight Crosby, professor of the history of art, and Carroll L. V. Meeks, associate professor of architecture. Mr. Curtis' meticulous reading of my text prepared the way for considerable stylistic improvement in the ultimate draft. Mr. Crosby played a most important part in arranging for publication by the Yale University Press. To Mr. Meeks I owe a special debt of gratitude. Some years ago we pooled all our graphic documentation on railway stations and a large part of the illustrations in chapters XV and XVI come from his files although it is the ultimate sources that are indicated in the List of Illustrations. I must also mention the continuous assistance of the staff of the Sterling Library at Yale; if this book was written from the resources of any other library than my own, it was that of Yale. In particular the willingness of the Sterling authorities to allow vast quantities of books and periodicals to be transported to Meriden, Connecticut, and kept there for weeks on end explains the high quality of the line illustrations which the Meriden Gravure Company could thus make directly from original wood engravings and other contemporary plates. Without this remarkable cooperation the high standard of the Yale Press in the matter of illustration copy could not have been maintained.

The expression of further obligations must be categorized: first, financial assistance; second, sources of information; third, access to buildings; fourth, illustrative material; fifth, reprinted material; sixth, technical assistance, etc.

Although much desultory research had been done before the war, work on this book really started with the opportunity to spend nine months in England in 1945–46 on a fellowship provided by the John Simon Guggenheim Memorial Foundation. While at Wesleyan University I was assisted by several generous research grants. A considerable contribution deriving from the estate of Isabel Paul of Newfields, N. H., helped to make publication possible.

With few exceptions, the writers whose books and articles are cited in the text have also notably assisted by providing information in conversation or in letters. Mr. Summerson's important aid has already been mentioned; that of H. S. Goodhart Rendel, perhaps the best informed person in England on Victorian architects in general, Nikolaus Pevsner, Carroll Meeks, Turpin C. Bannister, Graham C. Law, John Betjeman, J. M. Richards, Marcus Whiffen, and Phoebe Stanton should also be signalized. To the successive librarians of the Royal Institute of British Architects, Edward J. Carter, R. E. Enthoven, and James Palmes, who made available the resources of the world's finest architectural library, warm thanks are also due; and, in the United States, to the librarians of architecture and planning of the Massachusetts Institute of Technology and of Harvard University.

It is impossible even to list all the clergymen and institutional authorities who have facilitated access to buildings in their charge, frequently providing useful information as well. But I can take this opportunity to express my gratitude to the late Duke of Montrose, the Duke of Sutherland, Lord Carnarvon, and Lord Rosebery for the privilege of visiting their houses; and also to Lord Amulree for arranging for me to see in great detail, up to the very iron roofs, the Houses of Parliament. I would also like to thank those who, alas unavailingly, attempted to obtain entree to Balmoral Castle for me. How many terrace houses in London of the Victorian period I have at one time or another been inside is hard even to estimate; nor yet can I hope to enumerate all those friends and acquaintances whose dwellings have provided so much of the background of knowledge and experience on which certain aspects of the account of housing in Chapters XIV and XV are based.

A very large proportion of the illustrations come from 19th-century books and periodicals in the author's possession, above all from the files of the *Builder* and the *Illustrated London News* which between them provide so splendid a pictorial coverage of building history for all but the very earliest years of the Early Victorian period. As many more are from publications in the Sterling Library. Harvard supplied a copy of Baron Ernouf's *Art des jardins* as well as several periodicals not in Sterling Library, and Smith College furnished a copy of A. E. Richardson's *Monumental Classic Architecture*. To Professor Richardson and his publishers, B. T. Batsford, thanks are due for permission to use five illustrations from the latter work. A group of photographers, J. R. Johnson of Western Reserve University, Annan of Glasgow, Turl of Bristol, and Palmer of Manchester, took photographs especially for this work—in the case of Mr. Johnson in very considerable numbers. The photographs of the Coal Exchange were taken by Helmut Gernsheim for the author's article in the *Architectural Review*, and I am most grateful to the editors of the *Review* for allowing their use here, as also to Professor Rudolf Wittkower of the Warburg Institute for allowing the use of the photographs Mr. Gernsheim took for the Institute of Bridgewater House. I should also mention several photographs by R. H. de Burgh-Galwey and by Dell and Wainwright, covered by the *Architectural Review's* copyright, which are used here with the editors' permission. Mr. Gernsheim also generously supplied a copy of one of the early Crystal Palace photographs; the rest of these, as well as those of the Brompton Boilers in construction, I was allowed to have copied from originals at the Victoria and Albert Museum. To the Museum authorities, and particularly to Mr. C. H. Gibbs-Smith, I am most grateful.

Sixteen illustrations are from photographs especially made for this book from drawings, watercolors and lithographs in the library of the Royal Institute of British Architects, and these are used here with the kind consent of the Institute. Paxton's original sketch of the Crystal Palace is reproduced from a photograph supplied by the Royal Society of Arts, with whom it is deposited. A Pugin drawing at Scarisbrick is reproduced from Michael Trappes-Lomax's *Pugin, a Mediaeval Victorian,* with the author's generous permission and that of his publishers Sheed and Ward. Five illustrations were provided by the British Railways, or their predecessors the Great Western Railway and the London and North Eastern Railway, largely through the generous interest of Brian Lewis and Christian Barman. I am most grateful to the Town Clerk of Birkenhead for providing a photograph of an early plan. Mr. Whiffen has allowed me to use two of his photographs, and there is one of Mr. Law's, whose study of "Greek Thomson" has appeared in the *Architectural Review* (*115*, 307–16) since the main text of this book went to press. Messrs. Drake and Lasdun, the architects who are rebuilding so much of Paddington, provided a photograph of Westbourne Grove. To the Yale University Art Gallery I am especially grateful for permission to reproduce the Paxton watercolor formerly belonging to John Carter, who has all along taken a flattering interest in this book.

The continued assistance of Walter Godfrey and Cecil Farthing of the National Buildings Record has supplied me with almost innumerable photographs of Victorian architecture, of which 83, as has been noted, are reproduced. Additional photographs come from Messrs. Salmon of Winchester, Hammond of Leamington, the late F. C. Inglis of Edinburgh, McCann of Uttoxeter, Tuck and Valentine of London, Garratt of Bristol, Jay of Cheltenham, and Pickard of Leeds. Some half dozen or more photographs unfortunately provided no evidence of source whatsoever and for them it is impossible to make acknowledgment.

A very considerable portion of Chapters XV and XVI appeared in a pamphlet, *The Crystal Palace, The Structure, Its Antecedents and Its Immediate Progeny* (Northampton, 1951; 2d ed. 1952), issued in connection with an exhibition prepared in 1951 by the Smith College Museum of Art and the Massachusetts Institute of Technology and still, in 1954, being circulated by the Smithsonian Institution. The author wishes to express his gratitude to the *Architectural Review* for allowing him to incorporate the bulk of his articles published in that journal on the "Coal Exchange," on "Victorian Monuments of Commerce," and on "Brunel and Paddington," as also some material from that on "Early Cast Iron Façades." I am also grateful to Georges Wildenstein for permitting the inclusion of my article "Second Empire 'avant la lettre'" which appeared in the *Gazette des Beaux Arts*. The epigraph preceding the Preface comes from a review of André Malraux's *Voices of Silence* by George Boas in *Perspectives U.S.A.*, No. 7, and is used with the permission of Mr. Boas.

To my colleagues Ruth Wedgwood Kennedy, Phyllis Williams Lehmann, and Mary Bartlett Cowdrey, I am grateful for discussion of various technical points concerning the text; and most notably to Miss Cowdrey for advice and assistance in the preparation of the index. In the last six years Rita Halford has typed and retyped the manuscript so often she should know it by heart! Her devoted assistance in meeting a succession of deadlines has been supplemented by various members of the staff of the Smith College Museum of Art at times of particular stress. Alan Brooks, a graduate student at Yale,

ACKNOWLEDGMENTS

undertook the job of getting the books and periodicals out of the Sterling Library to be sent to Meriden.

No teacher can terminate a list of acknowledgments like this without mentioning his students. At Wesleyan University, at the Massachusetts Institute of Technology, at Smith College, at the Institute of Fine Arts of New York University, and at Yale large portions of the material in this book have been presented in seminars or lecture courses. The opportunity thus to put the results of research before intelligent and interested younger people is one no scholar should be without. More particularly I should like to mention, among my Yale students, Robert W. Duemling, Wilder Green, John Hoag, and James Evans, and among my New York University students, Ellen Kramer: Their researches have often paralleled or complemented my own, and discussion with them has always been of great value.

Finally, and not least, are certain friends, no specialists in 19th-century architecture, who have yet often accompanied me in London and through the British countryside in pursuit of buildings they sometimes thought totally unappetizing. I hope that Ivan Brodrick and Arthur O'Malley-Williams, in reading this book, will see how the various things we visited fit into place.

The length of this acknowledgment section—and, long as it is, I am only too sure it inadvertently omits many who have, in the last decade, signally aided me in one way or another—expresses the cooperative nature of historical research in the arts. Without financial assistance of various sorts, without libraries and photograph collections, without discussion with other scholars, without hospitable owners, without friends, colleagues, and students to aid and to comfort, no such work as this could well be completed.

CONTENTS

CHAPTER I: THE STUDY OF

VICTORIAN ARCHITECTURE

"If the seed die not . . . ," it is written in the Bible; and sometimes, with buildings as with other artifacts of any particular period, only the loss of a large part of the finest work leads to recognition of the value and interest of what remains. For the student of Victorian architecture, as for the historian of any other aspect of the 19th century, the quantity and the availability of extant material are almost an embarrassment. Despite the blitz there is still much more building of the Victorian Age left in Britain than there is of any earlier period—perhaps even of all earlier periods together. In studying Victorian architecture seriously it is almost as important to decide what not to look at—or better what not to look for—as it is to consider the monuments of the age critically and historically at all.

The immediate Late Georgian background of the Early Victorian period will be discussed in the next chapter; here a different sort of preparation is needed: some discussion of the "how," if not so explicitly of the "why," of studying Victorian architecture. The Victorian Age well knew that its most conspicuous buildings were not always its best. In quality a surprising disparity exists between the large and obvious Victorian monuments of the 1870's—the Law Courts in London, say, or the town halls of the North—and earlier and generally more modest edifices which are little noticed today. Many of the former were built long after the several different kinds of Victorian design they exemplify were well past their prime, even though their architects had once been capable of really fine things. Too many critics base their judgment of Victorian architecture solely on these later monuments, so often worse than overripe, because the earlier work is inadequately known or less assertive in the urban scene.

Many of the finest examples of Victorian architecture have to be sought out in obscure places; even when found they require from the observer some effort of the historical imagination if they are to be properly appreciated. A book on Victorian architecture must therefore tell where the most significant edifices are to be found and also provide some explanation of their original cultural context. Even more important is the marshaling of a profusion of illustrative material; thus only can the generic image of what is

1

Victorian, which most people already recognize, be made more specific. Carefully selected monuments, thoroughly studied, should provide the basis for judgments of Victorian architecture, not blurred impressions of buildings glimpsed from a train or casually passed in the streets. Many excellent 19th-century edifices are never properly perceived today. Although Victorian work may be recurrently seen in its present shabby state, unless a conscious attempt is made by the observer to consider the builders' intentions, as well as to re-create in imagination the pristine condition and the original surroundings, much of it remains effectively as invisible as ruins still unexcavated.

Victorian buildings, it must be admitted, have not on the whole aged graciously. Perhaps this is merely because they are not yet quite old enough; more probably it is because their predominantly metropolitan sites expose them to excessive visual hazards in the way of surface grime and domineering later neighbors. The most admired productions of other ages, medieval castles and cathedrals, country mansions of the Tudor and Stuart ages, or residential squares and crescents of Georgian times have more often been spared such hazards or else have been completely destroyed. Victorian buildings are hard enough to see at first hand without a visual filter; somehow one's eyes must penetrate the grime that covers them and succeed also in shutting out the taller and brighter neighbors on either side. But 19th-century edifices are harder still to photograph satisfactorily; and most of us, alas, are conditioned to believe about architecture only what the camera records. Since the earlier Victorian monuments are less strident than the later ones, and more readily mistaken for Georgian, the lens often seems to miss their most characteristic virtues, and sometimes even to push them back a full generation in time. Too often the photographer himself has not recognized work of the 40's for what it is, but seen only quaintness and decay or an old-maidish sort of primness.

All Victorian buildings are in some sense on trial; their historian, however objective he might prefer to be, is therefore like a defense attorney before a diffident or hostile jury. The frequent use of contemporary pictures in this book may seem a little like producing childhood photographs of hardened criminals in the hope of swaying a jury in their favor; yet such pictures are most necessary if the subject of Early Victorian architecture is to be properly covered at all. Contemporary photographs of buildings of the late 30's, the 40's, and the early 50's are surprisingly hard to find; this despite the fact that calotypy and daguerreotypy were available from almost the beginning of the Victorian Age and more modern methods of photography from shortly after 1850. (Architecture, moreover, was a particularly good subject for the camera in days when exposures were unconscionably long.)

In the absence of early photographs other contemporary visual documents have very great value; the wood engravings of the 50's, moreover, were frequently based on photographs. The illustrations in the professional and general periodicals of the Victorian Age provided the means by which architectural ideas were spread as well as the images on which contemporary taste was formed. On them, furthermore, most contemporaries were forced to base their aesthetic judgments. Once one learns to interpret the documents a magic key is available to the architectural vision of the time such as line engravings of the 17th and 18th centuries provide for those earlier periods. If it is proper to appreciate Georgian architecture in the engraved plates of Colen Campbell and Robert Adam—and 18th-century design can hardly be understood without careful study of such plates—it is even more profitable to utilize the wealth of visual documentation which has come down from the Victorian Age.

An extremely rapidly flow of influence, not only within the British Isles but across the seas to the Dominions and the United States, characterized the whole Victorian Age and particularly its earlier decades. The speed with which submovements within the principal stylistic developments ran their course, from their first isolated introduction to their ultimate vulgarization, is both explained and chronicled by the contemporary visual documents. As in our own day, the effect of the design of a particular building on the general course of development did not have to await its completion, or sometimes even its initiation.

A present-day photograph of a Victorian building when labeled only with the original date of the architect's design or the date of its completion is likely to offer rather uncertain evidence as to the true place of that building in the history of 19th-century architecture. Pictures of the Houses of Parliament are often glibly dated "1837" (Fig. I 1), although Sir Charles Barry (1795–1860) * redesigned most of that enormous complex in the 40's and final completion, under the supervision of his son Edward Middleton Barry (1830–1880), came only well after his death in the mid-60's. The contemporary published view of Barry's Athenaeum in Manchester showed the original project (Fig. I 3), not the executed building (Fig. I 2) which is slightly different. In such situations contemporary graphic documents are obviously essential both to understand the architect's intention and to assess the possible effect of his original design as an influence on the work of others.

The available wealth of contemporary documentation in the form of plans,

---

* The points in the text where the principal biographical facts concerning important Early Victorian architects are given may be found by referring to the Index. Dates of birth and death will be supplied whenever possible where significant works by the various architects are first discussed.

sections, and technical details of construction offers advantages to the historian that are unobtainable for most earlier periods except through the preparation of modern measured drawings. It may not be so evident that wood engravings of details whose interest is visual rather than intellectual provide as good (or better) evidence as do photographs. The 20th century has come to accept photographs so naturally as substitutes for reality that much of our architecture is accused of being "photogenic": that is, designed to be appreciated more in photographs than in actuality. The parallel accusation that Victorian architecture was designed in considerable part to be appreciated in the reproductive media of the day is of course at least as true. For that reason, and because the judgment of all architecture, old or new, was necessarily based on familiarity with monuments studied through these media, contemporary illustrations have a special sort of psychological accuracy. They show what the architects intended—and also what the contemporary observer must have apprehended—far better than any photographs, even early photographs, can do.

The changing character of the visual documents may also be used to discriminate among the successive phases of Victorian style. Lithographs were used mostly in books rather than in periodicals (Fig. I 6); but in their delicacy of tonal contrast and their soft contours lithographs are perhaps truer to the architectural vision of the late 30's and early 40's than such simple outline drawings (Fig. I 4) and crudely vignetted perspectives (Fig. I 5) as could then be reproduced by the wood engravers working for the periodicals. By the 50's, however, with the rapid and climactic improvement in reproductive wood engraving, the qualities of the best illustrative craftsmanship came to parallel very closely the special qualities of the most characteristic new buildings. Bold black and white patterning and vigorous, rather than subtle, linear definition are successfully combined with strong illusions of three-dimensionality and coloristic rather than textural distinction of materials (Fig. XVII 5) to produce expressive images of the buildings of the day as contemporaries were seeing them.

Photography had by the 50's impinged considerably upon wood-engraving technique; for the camera had already set new standards of perspective presentation and of formalized value rendering. By then, moreover, the camera was often providing the intermediary documents from which wood engravers worked. But that development occurred, of course, only at the end of the Early Victorian period, and we are concerned here with its beginnings.

When *did* the Early Victorian period in architecture begin? "When" in cultural history, unless it be explained in terms of "how" and "why"—and also "where"—has little significance. The locus in the present instance presents no difficulty, since the scene has been set by definition in Great Britain. Few would deny that the United States had a Victorian Age in architecture quite as certainly as it had a Georgian one; and English Victorian influence was certainly not without importance elsewhere. But Victorian architecture had first to come into existence at home before it could be exported. The "why" and the "how" can be explained only with a broad preliminary examination of the British architectural scene in the 30's; more detail will be given in the next chapter.

Early in 1837 Sir John Soane (b. 1753), Architect of the Bank of England, died. His intransigent originality had perturbed the academic complacency of the profession for a full half-century. Yet in the 20th century he is often rated as the only Georgian architect later than Robert Adam (1728–1792) who belongs in the very first rank of achievement. Abroad only Karl Friedrich Schinkel (1781–1841), a generation younger, was his equal in distinction within his lifetime. Whether Soane's reputation ought to rival that of Sir Christopher Wren, as it does in many circles today, is a matter of taste; but that he was the greatest English architect of the High Romantic period can hardly be disputed, however much he may have owed to his first master, the younger George Dance (1744–1825). Soane, unlike Dance, was one of the few architects of the day whose production continued during the Napoleonic Wars almost unhampered by political and economic events. He could not, therefore, have many serious rivals in Europe between 1790 and 1815; and the New World was hardly yet ripe to produce architects of its own of so high a rank, even though the United States acquired in Latrobe its first professional, and one of great talent, at this very time.

Soane's death, therefore, rather than the accession of a 17-year-old female sovereign later in the same year, makes 1837 memorable in architectural history. But neither event need have signalized the termination of an architectural epoch in England, much less the opening of a new one. The final ending of individual careers, however distinguished, and the opening of new reigns, however prolonged, rarely mark except by coincidence major changes of historical phase in architecture.

Looking at early 19th-century cultural developments in Germany or France, a comparable change of phase—from High Romanticism to Late, from the world of David and Beethoven to that of Delacroix and Berlioz— seems to have come in 1830, a year of revolution in literature and the arts as well as in politics. In England also one might be led to select a date in the early 30's on political if not on musical or literary grounds, and various writers have done so. The crucial event would be not the death in 1830 of the last of the four Georges (which was so smoothly followed by his brother William's accession) but the stormy passage of the first Reform Act in 1832; for the passage of the act constituted a bloodless revolution from which the Victorian Age was to derive its special political character. But the reign of William IV lasted only a brief seven years, and the full results of the act's extension of

5

the franchise were hardly felt before those years were over and William's niece established upon the throne. Events more directly related to building production must decide when the Victorian Age really began in architecture.

Soane built little in the 30's. As far as one can judge, now that almost none of his late work remains, that little was neither of the high quality nor of the assured originality of his earlier production of the period 1790–1830. The State Paper Office, in Duke Street, St. James's, for example, seems not to have continued any one of his established stylistic lines; rather it paralleled the new "Italian palace" mode that the young Charles Barry was introducing at the same time in the Travellers' Club house nearby in Pall Mall (Fig. I 7). The Law Courts at Westminster appear to have been virtuoso spacial compositions exploiting hanging vaults. But these represent, one must suppose, rather the willful diversions of an old master, delighting to shock the younger generation, than any advance beyond the superb interiors at the Bank of England.

Soane, for all his official appointments—or perhaps, such is professional jealousy, because of them—had long stood apart from most of his contemporaries, both younger and older, somewhat as does Frank Lloyd Wright in 20th-century America. Encomiums of a high order were finally granted him by the profession when he received a special gold medallion from the Royal Institute of British Architects in 1835, two years after retiring from a 45-year term as Architect of the Bank. But many of these tributes resembled, in their evident insincerity, those that Wright received from the American Institute of Architects in 1949 after 56 years of distinguished practice. The savor of this belated (and rather hypocritical) recognition from the middle generation, moreover, was soon soured by the biting satire of the youthful A. N. W. Pugin (1812–1852) in his *Contrasts*, which appeared the next year.

As if with some premonition of the short life which many of his principal buildings were destined to have, Soane devoted his last years to making a museum of his London house. No other architect has taken such care to insure that his ideas shall continue manifest to later generations. But it was to be almost a century before architects and critics began to appreciate his bequest; even today it is little more than a curiosity to the general public. To an amazing extent, despite the Soane Museum, Soane's fame died with him.

Of Soane's last two pupils one, George Bailey, became the first curator of the museum and effectively ceased practice. The other, Charles J. Richardson (1800–1872), was also drawn into the museum project, for it was he who provided the attractive lithographed plates in the monograph on the museum Soane published in 1835. But Richardson was already busy on his own with *A Popular Treatise on the Warming of Buildings* (1837, with two later editions) and, more significant¹y, with the preparation of a series of meticulously accurate lithographic plates of Elizabethan and Jacobean architecture which he began to publish in separate parts at about the same time. His *Observations on the Architecture of England during the Reigns of Queen Elizabeth and King James I* came out as a book in 1837 and was one of the first of a series of similar works by him and others.

It is of particular interest that Richardson included in his publications, besides modern views and measured drawings, facsimiles of original plans and sketches. Here was something Greek and Gothic archaeologists are practically never able to supply, and such plates introduced a new sophistication into the presentation of the architectural styles of the past. The group of plates Richardson copied from Wendel Dietterlin's *Architectura* (Nuremberg, 1598), one of the continental sources on which the Elizabethan and Jacobean designers of ornament leaned heavily, is less surprising to find than the reproductions of drawings by John Thorpe, then supposed to have been a leading architect under Elizabeth. How ironical it is that these drawings, among the choicest items in Soane's extensive collection, should thus have provided the inspiration for so much anti-Soanic architecture.

The Dance Cabinet, the central shrine of Soane's library, preserves the remarkable projects of his revered friend and master, the younger Dance. These are, moreover, the evident source of many of Soane's most brilliant conceptions of architectural form. But the Dance drawings were to remain unstudied, by Richardson or anyone else, practically until our own day. The great Adam portfolios, from which Richardson made a few unpublished tracings, had to wait only until the late 70's to be appreciated.

Richardson's career, long and busy enough as writer, teacher, and architect, was in no way distinguished after this moment in the late 30's. He is the first Victorian architect there is occasion to discuss; yet the illustrations in his late book *The Englishman's House*, first published in 1870 and reissued in several later editions both English and American, show how little his architecture was to be affected by the characteristic developments of three Victorian decades. Remote though Richardson's house designs are from what the world generally recognizes as Georgian, most can be matched in the plates of cottage books that other architects issued before George IV's death. To the end, therefore, Richardson's work may be considered characteristically proto-Victorian rather than truly Victorian.

Elizabethan and Jacobean architecture was to Late Georgians and Early Victorians neither Classic nor Gothic; but, being a local English amalgam of both, was deemed more "national" than either. Interest in old work of around 1600 was no novelty by the 1830's, moreover. Nikolaus Pevsner has lately shown (*Architectural Review, 107,* 117–120) that at one end of the 18th century Sir John Vanbrugh (1664–1726) drew inspiration from early 17th-century planning; and that at the other end Richard Payne Knight (1750–1824) used an unmistakably Elizabethan or Jacobean design to illustrate his Picturesque ideal of a country mansion in a naturalistically landscaped setting. But in the High Romantic period of the late 18th and early 19th centuries such design had not yet acquired the prestige or the popularity of the "Grecian" or the "Gothick"; nor had there been earlier attempts to document its monuments with any care. This new interest in the English architecture of the late 16th and early 17th centuries in the 30's was therefore especially significant of the approaching end of the Georgian rule of taste.

Among Soane's pupils of Richardson's generation only George Wightwick (1802–1872) in provincial Plymouth retained a place for the "Soanic" among the multiple stylisms he employed. Perhaps Soane's manner of design was too personal to be further developed by others and could only thus survive as an obsolescent variant of Late Georgian Classicism. However that may be, Soane's "modernism" was abjured even before his death as absolutely as the innovations of the Arts and Crafts group in England and of the Chicago School in America were rejected in the resurgent "traditionalism" that followed the first World War. Not until the 50's, when originality was once more vaunted, did critics find a good word to say for this "Boeotian"; for Boeotian was the name Soane's early enemies applied to him in a supposedly "Athenian" age. (He sued for libel but lost the case.)

The term "Victorian" is in some ways as meaningful—and should be as neutral—a stylistic designation in architecture as "Georgian"; certainly it ought not to be used as a libelous term. The accession of Victoria herself was, however, even less·relevant to the change of phase in architecture than the death of Soane. Some at least of her Hanoverian forebears had been enthusiastic patrons of the arts; almost as a matter of principle she was not. Her personal tastes had in fact nothing at all to do with establishing the "Victorian" character of the architecture of her time.

Although in the course of two decades the actual settings in which the Queen lived became Victorian enough, her own tastes seem to have acted as a brake on those responsible for creating those settings. Yet she had neither the active interest nor the serious training to make her remain a convinced Georgian in the way of many leading aristocrats throughout the first part of her reign. The laggard manner in which she accepted new modes and the early death in 1862 of the Prince Consort, to whose judgment she had always turned in matters of art, insured that her surroundings remained Early Victorian, if in a rather commonplace way, to the very end of her life in 1901. But they had actually begun to be so only in the late 40's and early 50's when Early Victorian modes were already well established generally.

Even the more cultivated Albert's various connections with matters architectural are of real significance only in relation to the Crystal Palace. More than his wife he was led by personal inclination—and in conscious emulation of his Royal German contemporaries, of course—to take a rather direct interest, even to "dabble," in the arts. But duty seemed to require that he devote the greater part of his time to affairs of state. His own cautiousness, if not suggestions from the avuncular Baron Stockmar or from English associates, warned him of the unfavorable public reaction that could follow upon conspicuous expenditure by a mere consort of funds grudgingly voted by Parliament for Royal use.

The sort of Victorian taste the various Royal residences illustrate can be, without injustice, described as provincial or even suburban. Like the rather similar mansions which the rising provincial magnates were building in the suburbs of the Northern and Midland cities, the new portions of Buckingham Palace (Figs. IX 1–6) and the private retreats of the Sovereign on the Isle of Wight (Figs. VI 22–23) and in the Highlands (Figs. VIII 25–28) represent in their stylistic character a lag of a decade or more behind such architectural developments as were being patronized by the cultural elite. But for the exalted station of the clients, these houses would be almost beneath the notice of posterity. Only perhaps at the Home Farm near Windsor Castle, where Albert was eventually his own master, are there hints of an early response to "high" fashion in design.

In less private architectural matters into which the Prince was drawn, such as the campaign for the internal decoration of the Houses of Parliament (Chapter IX), the building for the Great Exhibition of 1851 (Chapter XVI), and the sponsorship of low-cost workers' housing (Chapter XIII), Albert's artistic tastes are less evident than his scientific and social enthusiasms. Choosing usually as his closest associates distinguished Victorians whose achievement was only incidentally related to architecture, he generally received advice that was more competent technically than aesthetically. Important though Albert's relation to Victorian building is, at least compared with his wife's, and particularly so in the early 50's, the architecture of the mid-century need not be called "Albertine." Neither his appearance on the English scene in the early 40's nor his death twenty years later can be correlated closely with architectural events.

It is convenient to divide the Victorian Age as a whole into successive periods, with one break in the early 50's and another around 1870. The architectural production of such short periods should not be considered to illustrate wholly distinct style-phases. But to confuse these style-phases or to merge them, as did those Victorians who wrote about the Victorian Age primarily in terms of a continuous "Gothic Revival," is to make more difficult rather than to simplify the problem of defining Victorian architecture as a whole. In certain fields of building—usually those fields in which self-consciousness about style was least cultivated by the Victorians—the continuity between the three subperiods is nearly unbroken. In such fields the stylistic breaks came so gradually and so belatedly that visual appearance often provides only ambiguous indexes for dating; yet the fact that most surface modulations did in the end reach all sorts of building production shows how unified the Victorian architectural world really was. A conscious snobbery may have set professional architects apart from mere builders as lawyers were set apart from their clerks; there were even within the profession itself diverse social categories as complex and mysterious as those stratifying the middle classes in county towns. But Victorian attitudes toward social status never seriously inhibited the flow of architectural ideas from one realm of building to another, although they undoubtedly made it rather slow and uneven.

To determine when the Victorian Age began one must have some idea as to when the Late Georgian period ended; for to recognize and attempt to characterize a seven-year "Williamite" phase of transition between is unprofitable (the term, in any event, is a barbarism). Precisely during those seven years, however, various cultural phenomena, mostly with roots deep in the 18th century but hitherto merely exceptions to more dominant patterns, developed a new sort of vigor. At last these forces were able to break through the general restraint imposed by the Georgian rule of taste that had so long held sway.

As in the case of the loose alliance of various contradictory political interests that passed the Reform Act, the supporters of new ideas in architecture, after gaining the upper hand in tacit concert, began to war lustily among themselves. Throughout the Early Victorian period what actually superseded the old rule of taste was no more, on the surface, than an uneasy eclecticism; yet under this variegated eclecticism certain visual criteria did hold general sway, even if no articulate body of doctrine concerning architecture was adumbrated. The writers of the day, so much less clear minded than those of the 18th century, had little ability or even desire to recognize and define these general criteria—in justice it must be admitted the task is not an easy one—since the nature of criticism was growing increasingly antivisual and absolutist at this very time.

The major new aesthetic categories recognized in the late 18th century represented the private attempts of a few highly cultivated connoisseurs to explain qualities which they thought desirable in the various arts even though those qualities were contrary to inherited concepts of "beauty." After nearly two generations these new categories were widely, if often implicitly, accepted. The visual concept of the Picturesque (though not so much that of the Sublime) had long been propagated by poets and novelists. Thus that concept was at least partially understood by all the articulate upper and middle classes (as I suppose the "nonrepresentational" or "abstract" is in the arts today). But in gaining wider currency, the idea of the Picturesque also lost precision. Almost anything might be considered picturesque, provided it was different from the standard productions of the previous age. The reaction against Georgian taste in the second quarter of the 19th century, once it had spread through the literate community, produced at first therefore a rather frivolous libertinism in the arts; yet within the frothy range of up-to-date architectural fashions hard centers of purpose were beginning to solidify by the mid-30's. These nodes of absolutist theory provided early evidence that the middle decades of the 19th century would not, in fact, be at all frivolous but rather deadly in their seriousness about the arts.

The rather sudden consolidation of the most earnest of these nuclei of purpose in the mature Gothic Revival around 1837 is often thought to epitomize the beginning of Victorian architecture. But to assign prime significance thus to one aspect only of the architectural scene, even to the Gothic Revival in its Puginian and Camdenian phases, cannot adequately explain the wide variety of types of design which actually characterizes building production in the late 30's and 40's. To do so, moreover, is to blame a few cranks and purists for a general confusion of taste they were in fact loudest in denouncing.

The third chapter of this book is devoted to "Pugin as a Church Architect," and the two that follow deal principally with the church builders who were his Anglican emulators. But that is so chiefly for reasons of dramatic organization. Such primacy of position must not be construed as a confirmation of the theory that assigns prime importance only to Gothic church building in the story of Early Victorian architecture. Following on those three chapters on church architects the next two are devoted to Barry's Italian palaces and their emulation by others in various fields of secular building.

Already introduced in the 20's, the *palazzo* manner (so to call it) had a considerably earlier start than did Pugin's Gothic, although it was not widely used, even by Barry himself, before the last years of the next decade. Once firmly rooted about the time of Victoria's accession, this 16th-century Italian mode remained as popular in England through the 40's and 50's as the 14th-century English mode of Pugin's churches. On the Continent a parallel manner was much more generally utilized. Thus some sort of revived Renaissance design, rather than the more exclusively English revived Gothic, must be considered the principal stylistic vehicle of Late Romantic architecture in general, of which the Early Victorian is merely the English variant.

11

The primarily stylistic preoccupations in these early chapters will be unsympathetic to many modern minds, but the terminology of the "revivals" can hardly be avoided if Early Victorian attitudes toward architecture are to be adequately presented. To balance these first five chapters, the next group deals largely with various building types rather than with surface stylisms. This section culminates in a discussion of those areas of building in which technical progress in construction rather than interstylistic strife was the chief preoccupation of the builders, whether they were engineers or architects or gardeners. To many Victorian leaders such a sequence, from the churches of Pugin to the Crystal Palace of the gardener Paxton, would have seemed a descent from the sublime to the all-but-ridiculous. To many modern readers, on the other hand, it is Pugin and his admirers who will seem ridiculous, not Paxton and his engineer associates Fox and Henderson. Let such, however, withhold their judgment awhile, for it is impossible to understand the Victorian Age unless the evangelistic purposes of the revivalists and the utilitarian motives of the technicians are fairly balanced and the entire work and thought of both honestly examined. Paxton, when building with conventional materials, was always an eclectic stylist; it was Pugin who was in theory a rigid "functionalist." (In practice, of course, he was inhibited by a lack of respect for functions and materials not closely similar to those familiar in medieval churches; but he did not hesitate to criticize the Crystal Palace on purely structural grounds.)

Pugin and Paxton are equally central figures in the picture of Victorian architecture, balanced like Plato and Aristotle in Raphael's "School of Athens." Knowledge of the two of them, both of what they really stood for and of what they in fact were able to accomplish, is as necessary to later architectural theorists as is knowledge of both Plato and Aristotle to philosophers. Pugin was much the more articulate of the two and his leadership began earlier and lasted longer. It is logical to present him first, even though Paxton's first great greenhouse (Fig. XV 29) was built as early as Pugin's first important church (Figs. III 6–9). Professionally speaking, Paxton was never either an architect or an engineer, much less an architectural critic. On the other hand the lively polemics of Pugin have confused rather than clarified later estimates of him as an architect and builder.

Both Pugin's theories and his mature achievement mark a turning point in the program of re-using medieval architectural forms which goes back to the mid-18th century. His mature emulation of 14th-century Gothic, with its ascetic rejection of all the later medieval fripperies which had delighted successive generations of Georgians, early established new standards for advanced church architects. His books of the late 30's and early 40's provided the basis for rigid new principles of "correct" Gothic building to which the new generation subscribed. But actually Thomas Rickman (1776–1841), a Quaker pharmacist turned medieval archaeologist, had preceded Pugin in several ways as a serious reformer of Georgian neo-Gothic. Even the accepted names for the successive phases of English Gothic architecture—Early English, Decorated, and Perpendicular—had first been introduced by him in his archaeological writing. After building fairly competent imitation-Gothic churches for nearly twenty years, Rickman was in the mid-30's a much more expert practitioner than the young Pugin when Pugin turned (at much the same time and in much the same spirit) toward Catholicism and a more careful revival of Gothic building methods. Occasional churches built a decade earlier by other men, such as Edward Lacey Garbett's church of Holy Trinity at Theale in Berkshire, had a medieval vigor and solidity that Pugin almost never equaled, except perhaps in his own church of St. Augustine's, Ramsgate. The vigor of Garbett's detailing derives from a study of Salisbury Cathedral, the asymmetrical composition from the principles of the Picturesque. Late Georgian Gothic, particularly as applied to churches, demands a more careful investigation than it has yet received. Such investigation will probably tend to minimize the revolution in actual building methods that Pugin initiated; but it will hardly modify the novelty of Pugin's controlling attitude toward Gothic design. For the "Revival of Christian Architecture" at which he aimed was not merely a matter of taste or even of archeological correctness.

Earlier the Gothick (to continue to give it a Georgian spelling) had been for the most part a whimsical or a pedantic or sometimes merely an economical alternative to the dominant classical modes, little more serious than the concurrent Chinese or Turkish fancies. Now the cause of "Christian or Pointed" architecture became for Pugin an essentially religious crusade deeply imbued with values both ethical and sacramental. This transfer to the architectural field of Evangelical earnestness was widely accepted by most Anglicans within a very few years—though *not* by those whose religious position was technically Evangelical. A comparable earnestness was henceforth the necessary moral garment of Victorian architectural leaders, however much they might, like the critic Ruskin, profess to scorn Pugin and his productions. Pugin's campaign thus provides a peculiarly topical subject with which to begin the Victorian story, even though only a relatively small part of Early Victorian architectural production was affected by his books and his way of building.

But an equally characteristic "Renaissance Revival," under Barry's unfanatical leadership, continued throughout the Early Victorian period to have a wider influence on general building production than Pugin's Gothic Revival. Barry and the other exponents of Renaissance design were less

13

drastic than the Gothic men in their rejection of established Georgian ways of seeing and ways of building. Generally latitudinarian in all things and not at all nationalistic, these men tended to accept the modern world much as they found it. Although hardly utilitarians in a strictly Benthamite sense, they envisaged for 19th-century architecture a progressive sequence of modulations. Serving new functional needs with real sympathy and freely utilizing new materials and structural methods, the Renaissance practitioners were above all moderates: Whigs or Liberals in political terms, not Tories or Radicals. To acquire credit in their ranks no such patterns of repentance and and conversion were demanded as by Pugin and the Camdenians. The "traditional" architects of the early 20th century were the natural heirs of such Victorians in their cool professionalism, their worldliness, and their accommodating approach to their clients' needs—as also, for that matter, often enough in their actual designing.

Renaissance men had no less scorn than Gothic Revivalists for most of the production of the earlier Georgian Age and gladly renounced as well the Grecian rigidities of the preceding decades. Yet there was a real continuity in the way the main structural and visual problems of architecture were approached. The Renaissance men belonged, more or less consciously, to the academic line that went back in England two centuries and more to Inigo Jones quite as much as to the broader international current to whose 15th- and 16th-century fountainheads they were programmatically returning.

W. H. Leeds (1786–1866) was the first, in the introduction to his monograph on Barry's Travellers' Club house, to provide a full-dress defense of the Renaissance case (*The Travellers' Club House . . . Accompanied by an Essay on the Present State of Architectural Study, and the Revival of the Italian Style* [1839]). Characteristically, he was much less fanatical in his attacks on Late Georgian practice than Pugin had been in his *Contrasts* three years earlier; he was also much less coherent and forceful in proposing a new set of architectural principles based on Renaissance practice. This Renaissance movement, although characteristic of the Early Victorian style-phase from the very first, does not therefore, in the precise way of Pugin's so much more concentrated Gothic campaign, fix the opening of the Victorian Age at any particular moment in time. The 19th-century Renaissance Revival, moreover, was never so closed and consistent in its doctrine or so exclusive in its professional membership as was the Gothic Revival from Pugin's time down at least to the 70's. Yet as Barry's leadership became generally accepted in the 40's the palaces of early 16th-century Rome more and more replaced those of late 16th-century Vicenza as models for various sorts of secular edifices, and these models were widely emulated well down into the 50's and beyond.

The beginning of the Victorian Age in the late 30's brought the wide acceptance of new stylistic models, English or Italian, and a parallel rejection of stylistic originality as an acceptable architectural aim. A new attitude toward the whole problem of architectural style in "modern" times was also taking shape. This attitude is really more significant than are the new stylistic models themselves or the general distrust of innovation. Without citing the examples which later chapters of this book will present in considerable profusion the attitude is rather hard to define. On the one hand, the styles of the past were considered to be vehicles for various general ideas; the novelty here is merely the association of different styles with different ideas, and even that had deep Georgian roots. Concepts of pure architectural form, such as are almost always necessary to aesthetic innovators, were generally ignored as mere Platonic abstractions: The forms of architecture were considered incapable of dissociation from the specific styles which had originally brought them into being. Yet it was also allowed that the formal elements of the various styles of the past could, within certain limits, be manipulated when they were "borrowed" for modern use, always provided that this manipulation was not alien to such definitions of the several styles as contemporary architectural historians were establishing. (These definitions are, of course, highly conventional ones and by no means coincide with those of the 20th century.) Thus it is the particular ways in which the forms of the past were manipulated by the Early Victorians that give the architecture of the period such homogeneity as it possesses.

That this new attitude toward style which took shape in the 30's did not lead merely to a kaleidoscopic eclecticism—as to many observers it seemed, and still seems, to have done—is largely due to the programmatic "revivals" or attempts to canalize 19th-century architecture within certain stylistic ranges. There were as yet no widely accepted ways of manipulating borrowed formal elements abstractly such as would begin to crystallize in the 50's (Chapter XVII). Of these more or less rigid programs for 19th-century architecture, Pugin's Gothic one and Barry's Renaissance one were, of course, the most influential. Quite as typical, however, is a third, of which Soane's pupil Richardson has already been mentioned as an early protagonist.

To refer to this third program as a "Jacobethan" revival is certainly convenient; the coined word, which is already current, neatly telescopes the later decades of the 16th century with the first decades of the 17th. But the term Jacobethan is more than a justifiable verbal convenience since the development of architecture in England was relatively continuous during the latter part of Elizabeth's reign and much of James I's, despite the change of dynasty. The major break began with Inigo Jones' first royal commissions around 1617; and that break was hardly complete, as regards architectural production as a whole, until well after the Civil War. Later Stuart

architecture of the sort which Jones initiated was to find few Victorian admirers and almost no emulators before the mid-50's.

To refer to the 16th–17th-century stylistic aspects of Early Victorian building production as a "revival" is questionable, however, for the Jacobethan
did not really "revive," that is, come to live again with a new life of its own,
even to the extent that the Gothic did with Pugin or the Renaissance with
Barry. Moreover, the Jacobethan Revival (so to call it all the same) was never
a major cultural movement throughout the whole Western world such as the
earlier Greek Revival had been in the preceding High Romantic period.
Yet this Jacobethan Revival is perhaps more definitely symptomatic of the
architecture of the whole Victorian Age, High and Late as well as Early—
if for somewhat different reasons in each case—than either the rabid Gothi-
cism of Pugin, on which attention is usually focused in studies of this period,
or the quite personal Italianism of Barry. In the general tradition of derivative
design in architecture, which lasted almost down to the present as an aftermath of the Victorian Age, the Jacobethan Revival likewise continued to have
a definite, if undistinguished, place. And on the Continent, above all in
France, parallel movements can readily be recognized in the 30's and 40's,
though they came rather later in Germany.

The obscure beginnings of the Jacobethan Revival in the 18th century are
only just being carefully studied by Pevsner and others. The Jacobethan was
certainly prominent, however, among the alternative stylisms offered in such
Late Georgian house-pattern books as P. F. Robinson brought out in the 20's
well before Richardson, Henry Shaw (1801–1873), and others had begun to
provide accurate documents for imitation. For Barry in the late 30's and 40's
a version he called "Anglo-Italian" once or twice provided a useful stylistic
vehicle. In 1836 Barry won the competition for the New Palace of Westminster with a Perpendicular project against competitors who interpreted
the "Gothic or Elizabethan" design demanded by the program in a Jacobethan
sense. At the same time he was confirming his personal predilection for the
Italian High Renaissance by winning the scarcely less important Reform
Club competition with a version of an early 16th-century Roman palace
(Figs. VI 4–6). But within a year he was also engaged on a project for rebuilding the Earl of Carnarvon's Georgian seat in Hampshire, Highclere
Castle, in an elaborate Jacobethan vein.

The building campaign at Highclere was slow to start and much prolonged, so that no illustration of it was published before that in the *Building
News* in 1858 (Fig. I 7), and Barry himself hardly ever utilized Jacobethan
forms again as such, except in restoring 17th-century mansions, any more
than he was to use the Perpendicular much outside his Westminster work.

On the other hand, many architects certainly seem to have emulated High-clere in the 40's and early 50's despite the fact that the design was not available in any book or periodical until so much later. The Jacobethan was so perfectly suited to the tastes of the Early Victorians and to the capacities of the building industry of the day that it would certainly have become popular even without the prestige of Highclere. However, there is a great difference between the general popularity of a given mode of design in any period and its real suitability to the creative capacities of the leading architects of the day. The neo-Jacobethan was very rarely as successful as at Highclere, and that fact was certainly widely recognized by architects if not by laymen in Victorian times. Paxton's Mentmore is the chief exception (Fig. VIII 24).

Men were naturally not aware in the late 30's that they would one day think of themselves as Victorians; hence no one then craved to establish a specifically "Victorian" style. Yet the more intelligent leaders of taste seem to have realized soon that they were no more cut out to be successful neo-Elizabethans than their fathers had been to be plausible neo-Grecians. Serious-minded men were naturally shocked by Elizabethan profligacy, which had nowhere been more evident than in the architecture of the time. The ease with which Jacobethan ornament could be produced in substitute materials like papier-mâché and cast stone roused justifiable suspicion; while the emphasis on ornament in the available books distracted attention from Jacobethan planning and fenestration, which might have been profitably emulated had as much been known about Hardwick as about Burleigh or Wollaton.

Among the less earnest Victorians, however, the Jacobethan had a vast success. It was much used for country houses, both new and remodeled, by landowners who suspected the fanaticism of the Gothicists as much as they did the cosmopolitanism of the Renaissance practitioners. The ornament also provided for schools, hospitals, and other institutional edifices a casual sort of surface embellishment that could be used in any quantity. This appealed as a contrast to the cold functional detailing of utilitarian buildings in the Late Georgian period, now hopelessly out of fashion even among the hard-headed members of charitable boards.

The hankering for this hybrid style of a great English age of the past was destined to continue well down into our own time. It is all the more significant, therefore, that even 20th-century architectural scholars have yet to arrive at a thorough and coherent explanation of the real character of Eliza-bethan and Jacobean design. Such an understanding the Victorians had achieved (or at least believed they had) for both Gothic and High Renais-sance design well before they came to emulate either with much aesthetic subtlety or creative vigor. But the Jacobethan, as John Steegman has pointed out in *Consort of Taste* (1950), was for them just "Olden Time," not a fully recognized style with a clearly definable character.

In the Early Victorian period the Jacobethan mode encouraged much less than did Gothic or Renaissance modes the creation of one of those illogical amalgams of archaeology and originality that alone give cultural vitality to a revival. Architects of neo-Jacobethan edifices rarely succeeded in fusing into a new alloy what they borrowed and what they added; the bronze-like idiosyncrasy of character which the best—and the worst—Victorian buildings in other modes so definitely possess was almost always lacking. When, in later Victorian times, characteristic elements from early 17th-century sources were successfully incorporated in a modern mode of design, these elements were rarely identified as Jacobethan. In the 70's and 80's Anne, not Elizabeth or James I, was the nominal Royal patron of the last Victorian revival that really revived.

The revived Jacobethan is generally an unsatisfactory 19th-century mani-festation. It is too typical of many of the Victorians' weaknesses and timidities, even if it is also highly symptomatic of certain of their strongest and most recurrent tastes in matters visual. Moreover the neo-Jacobethan is almost never novel in a creative way and hence could rarely be expressive of its time. Like the forgeries of earlier paintings or sculpture made in any period, the neo-Jacobethan helps to reveal what Victorians really liked; it certainly does not illustrate either the heights or the depths of which they were capable in architecture.

Harlaxton, a vast house near Grantham in Lincolnshire designed by Anthony Salvin (1799–1881), was begun before Highclere but even longer a-building. It is only too easy to mistake this pile, which out-Burleighs Bur-leigh House, for an authentic work of two centuries and more earlier—at least from a certain distance (Fig. I 9). That could never occur with the Italianate palaces or even with most of the English 14th-century Gothic churches that were built in the 40's and 50's. This remark is, of course, not intended as praise, for a work of art can express satisfactorily only its own age and no other. When means of expression are borrowed, as they fre-quently are in literature and music as well as in architecture, the justification for such loans does not lie in the artist's competence as a forger—which can rarely deceive for long—but in the new use the artist finds for what he has borrowed.

In the deepest sense the borrowed means of expression are not part of the form of the new work but rather part of what it expresses; that is, elements of its content or meaning. It is a convenience of speech to refer to "styles" in Victorian architecture, meaning the nominal vehicles of expression borrowed

18

from the styles of the past; but Victorian "style," in the best sense of that abused word, is something quite different. Harlaxton and all the other Jacobethan works of the age that half persuade us of their plausibility are in that sense all but devoid of style. Decade after decade the architects of country houses and of various sorts of institutions continued to work the Jacobethan vein with little or no change. But true style in art has life, of which the changes resulting from growth and development are the evidence; and only living style makes significant history. Little account will therefore be given in this book of Jacobethan production, since it maintained only a sort of vegetable existence. Other aspects of Early Victorian architecture came fully to life and teemed with bold actions and dramatic conflicts.

The new functional demands of the second quarter of the 19th century might seem today to have required an approach to design unconfused by stylistic preconceptions derived from the past. Yet in practice the need to create or develop new building types more often seemed to inhibit than to encourage conscious innovation in design as such. The workaday Victorian architects to whom these problems were usually consigned were neither particularly sensitive nor creative; their clients were likely to be frank Philistines. Railway stations, produce exchanges, and even museums, for example, were effectively new architectural types at this time; and for them surprisingly successful (though quite illogical) stylistic expression was often found by run-of-the-mill architects using almost accidental combinations of new materials and old forms. Whether the forms were cinquecento Italian or trecento Gothic, the results generally have a peculiarly 19th-century vigor.

Many modern critics see a different central dilemma in 19th-century architecture from that produced by the continuous "wars of the styles" for which Victorian critics were always mobilized. Foreign versus native, Gothic versus Renaissance, eclectic versus revivalist, evolutionary versus revolutionary, "copyistic" versus "real," moral or "Christian" Pointed versus worldly and "Pagan" Italian—all such verbalisms these critics would throw out as irrelevant in order to concentrate our attention almost solely on functional changes and structural developments. The story of the successive technical advances in construction in England from the mid-18th century on, particularly as regards the prefabrication of building elements and the increasingly bold use of ferrous products, could be most profitably told; but it would be a division of the general history of science and its applications, not an account of *architecture* as that art has generally been understood.

The portion of the technical story devoted to the period 1835–55, for example, would deal directly with only a few aspects of many of the most characteristic (not to say the most famous) Early Victorian monuments and would altogether omit many other rather important buildings. One need not accept any of the rigid definitions of architecture favored by the Victorians in order to feel that such a reduction of the significant building production of the mid-19th century to a few lines of evident "progress" in technics would be to ignore many of the legitimate aspirations of the best architectural minds of the age. Such a critical position repeats an error of one of those minds, that of Eugène-Emmanuel Viollet-le-Duc (1814–1879), who is so well known for a "rational" (more accurately, mechanistic) interpretation of the development of medieval architecture by now quite outdated.

Gothic architects and engineers in the Middle Ages operated (or so there is some reason to believe) more like scholastic philosophers than like modern technologists, just as might have been expected of the clerical world in which they lived. Engineers in the 19th century were almost as different from their 20th-century successors as from their medieval predecessors. On occasion 19th-century architects could produce better engineering-architecture than did their engineer rivals, work more comparable to the finest productions of the first real engineers, the men who were active just before the Victorian Age began.

Thomas Telford (1757–1834) and John Rennie (1761–1821) designed their stone bridges—and I mean "designed" in both the engineering and the architectural senses of the word—just as the ablest architects of their own Late Georgian day would have done. Engineering in masonry was still a part of architecture, and these men had been trained in architecture either by older architects or by self-instruction and experience. Scientific engineering theory was barely in its infancy, not an independent intellectual discipline.

The later 19th-century engineers were often poor architects. Isambard Kingdom Brunel (1806–1859), for example, in his Egyptian suspension bridge above the Clifton Gorge and in his castellated station at Temple Mead, two of the chief Early Victorian monuments of Bristol, echoed with enthusiasm the sillier stylisms of the day (Figs. XV 17, 20–21). The architect Francis Thompson's collaboration with Robert Stephenson (1803–1859) on the Britannia Tubular Bridge (Figs. XV 34–36, 38) and that of M. D. Wyatt with Brunel on Paddington Station (Figs. XVI 34–39), on the other hand, made of these far finer monuments than any that the Victorian engineers, who were generally without the sound architectural training of their Georgian predecessors, were capable of achieving on their own. Early Victorian engineering is partly separate from architecture, partly inextricably involved with it. To hypothesize a sequence of technical or engineering works uncorrupted by contemporary architectural ideals is only to dream—if indeed it is not consciously to falsify history in aid of a particular critical position of the present day.

If one wishes to give any serious consideration to Victorian architecture at all—an activity which appears now to occupy many critics and historians besides myself—it must be considered as a whole. The peculiar interest of the production of the period is not restricted to a few rather peripheral monuments of iron and glass like the Crystal Palace and the great railway sheds (Chapters XII and XIII). On the other hand to restrict one's study to the high-minded work of the Gothic Revivalists is equally wrong (Chapters III–V, XVII). The church builders enjoy the prestige of having been less loudly damned than most of their confreres by that great, if confused, Victorian architectural critic John Ruskin; but one must not take the Victorian scene at the Revivalists' own valuation any more than at Ruskin's.

Too much special pleading of various sorts, some of it inverted and ironic, has obscured the richness and vitality of the total Victorian story by concentrating attention on only one or another of its subplots. Early Victorian architecture, or all that matters of it, was not just the Gothic Revival, already the subject of several excellent books; nor was it merely some idealized "academic tradition" which even its admirers admit was much enfeebled after the 30's. Nor yet can Early Victorian architecture be restricted to the pure line of technical development, a line in any event not of uninterrupted progress but of bright hopes alternating with dismal slumps. Early Victorian architecture included all these things (and many others almost equally significant); it was in fact the sum of them, almost the result of their multiplication.

The many-voiced architectural music of the Victorian Age is complex in its orchestration after the harpsichord-like effects of the previous century. But it is the more intense dynamics of Victorian architecture even at its beginnings, characterized by crescendos and fortissimi rather than by soft passages, that remind us that this was the age of Berlioz in music as well as of the "Gothic Revival" of plainsong by the Benedictines. To understand Early Victorian architecture, and even perhaps to obtain from its special harmonies a pleasure no other age can provide, one must be ready to accept the piling up of large visual orchestras and choruses. A healthy suspicion of what both the 19th and the early 20th centuries have thought to be the "absolutes" of taste in the arts is also necessary.

An approach that is as charitable and uncensorious as that of the critics who have revived interest in later Roman architecture or in the divagations of style that followed the High Renaissance in Italy is required. The queasy attitude of those early 20th-century writers on the Victorian Age who tried to protect their own reputations for taste either by extreme selectivity or by excess of humorous reference should be avoided. I shall not eschew humor and occasionally must exhibit a touch of queasiness. But cold objectivity never did any humanistic subject good, however pathological its character; let us therefore laugh and be sick if we must, but as far as possible in concert with the Victorians. The 20th century certainly has no right to patronize the 19th.

ILLUSTRATIONS

23

II 9   Design for "Vicarage House." Elevation and plan from J. B. Papworth, *Rural Residences*, 1818.

II 10   Design for "Cottage Ornée." Perspective and plan from J. B. Papworth, *Rural Residences*, 1818.

II 11   Lodge, Villa Borghese, Rome. Perspective and plan from Charles Parker, *Villa rustica*, 1832.

II 12   Design for "Gothic Villa." By E. B. Lamb. From J. C. Loudon, *Encyclopedia of Cottage, Farm and Villa Architecture and Furniture*, 1833.

II 13   Design for "Gothic Villa." By E. B. Lamb. From *Architectural Magazine*, 1836.

II 14   Design for "Italian Villa." By E. B. Lamb. From *Architectural Magazine*, 1836.

II 15   Design for "Villa in the Cottage Style." From Francis Goodwin, *Domestic Architecture*, 1833.

II 16   Design for "Country Public House." By E. B. Lamb. From J. C. Loudon, *Encyclopedia of Cottage, Farm and Villa Architecture and Furniture*, 1833.

II 17   Royal Institution (now City Art Gallery), Mosley St., Manchester. By Sir Charles Barry, (1824) 1827–35.

II 18   St. Peter's Parish Church, Brighton. By Sir Charles Barry, (1823) 1824–28. Photo. N.B.R.

II 19   Travellers' Club House, Pall Mall, London. By Sir Charles Barry (1829) 1830–32. Garden front. Photo. N.B.R. Plan from W. H. Leeds, *The Travellers' Club House*, 1839.

II 20   Westminster New Palace, London. By Sir Charles Barry and A. N. W. Pugin, (1835–36) 1840–c.1865. Longitudinal section from *Building News*, 31 Dec. 1858.

II 21   Westminster New Palace, London. By Sir Charles Barry, A. N. W. Pugin and E. M. Barry, (1835–36) 1840–c.1865. Plan of principal floor from Alfred Barry, *Life and Works of Sir Charles Barry*, 1867.

II 22   Original design for Westminster New Palace, London. By Sir Charles Barry and A. N. W. Pugin, c.1836. South elevation from drawing at Royal Institute of British Architects.

II 23   Original design for Westminster New Palace, London. By Sir Charles Barry and A. N. W. Pugin, c.1836. North elevation from drawing at R.I.B.A.

II 24   Original design for Westminster New Palace, London. By Sir Charles Barry and A. N. W. Pugin, c.1836. West elevation from drawing at R.I.B.A.

II 25   Original design for Westminster New Palace. By Sir Charles Barry and A. N. W. Pugin. Perspective of river front, 1836. Photo. *Picture Post*.

II 26   King Edward's Free Grammar School, New St., Birmingham. By Sir Charles Barry, (1833) 1834–37. From Alfred Barry, *Life and Works of Sir Charles Barry*, 1867.

ILLUSTRATIONS

VI 19 Highclere Castle, near Burghclere, Hampshire. As refaced by Sir Charles Barry, (1837) 1842–44. Photo. Marcus Whiffen.

VI 20 Bury Athenaeum, New Market St., Bury, Lancashire. By Sydney Smirke, 1850–51. From *Builder*, 9 Nov. 1850.

VI 21 Mansion, Kensington Palace Gardens, London. By R. R. Banks, 1843. From Companion to the *British Almanac*, 1846.

VI 22 Osborne House, near East Cowes, I. of W. By Prince Albert and Thomas Cubitt. Private pavilion, 1845–46. Photo. *Picture Post*.

VI 23 Osborne House, near East Cowes, I. of W. By Prince Albert and Thomas Cubitt. Garden front, 1847–49. Photo. *Picture Post*.

VI 24 Harlaxton Hall, near Grantham. By Anthony Salvin, 1834–c.1855. Photo. *Country Life*.

VII 1 City of London Prison, Camden Road, Holloway, London. By J. B. Bunning, 1851–52. From *Builder*, 14 June 1851.

VII 2 Pentonville Prison, Caledonian Rd., London. By Sir Charles Barry, 1841–42. Plan from *Builder*, 9 Oct. 1847.

VII 3 Pentonville Prison, Caledonian Rd., London. By Sir Charles Barry, 1841–42. Entrance block from *Illustrated London News*, 7 Jan. 1843.

VII 4 Berkshire County Gaol, Reading. By Scott and Moffatt, 1842–44. From *Illustrated London News*, 17 Feb. 1844.

VII 5 Dunrobin Castle, near Golspie, Sutherlandshire. By Sir Charles Barry and Leslie of Aberdeen, (1844) 1845–48. From *Illustrated London News*, 14 Sept. 1872.

VII 6 Board of Trade, Whitehall, London. By Sir Charles Barry, 1845–47. From *Illustrated London News*, 24 Oct. 1846.

VII 7 Bridgewater House, Cleveland Sq., London. By Sir Charles Barry, 1847–57. Entrance front. Photo. Helmut Gernsheim.

VII 8 Bridgewater House, Cleveland Sq., London. By Sir Charles Barry, 1847–57. Plan from *Builder*, 13 Oct. 1849.

VII 9 Bridgewater House, Cleveland Sq., London. By Sir Charles Barry, 1847–57. Ceiling in large drawing room. Photo. Helmut Gernsheim.

VII 10 Bridgewater House, Cleveland Sq., London. By Sir Charles Barry, 1847–57. Green Park front. Photo. Helmut Gernsheim.

VII 11 Bridgewater House, Cleveland Sq., London. By Sir Charles Barry, 1847–57. Doorcase in large drawing room. Photo. Helmut Gernsheim.

VII 12 Bridgewater House, Cleveland Sq., London. By Sir Charles Barry, 1847–57. Picture gallery after blitz. Photo. Helmut Gernsheim.

VII 13 Dorchester House, Park Lane, London. By Lewis Vulliamy, 1848–63. Park front. Photo. N.B.R.

VII 14 Dorchester House, Park Lane, London. By Lewis Vulliamy, 1848–63. Plan from drawing at R.I.B.A.

VII 15 Dorchester House, Park Lane, London. By Lewis Vulliamy, 1848–63. Entrance court. Photo. N.B.R.

VII 16 Great Western Hotel, Conduit St. East, Paddington, London. By

VIII 16   Enbrook, near Folkestone. By S. S. Teulon, 1853–55. Perspective from *Builder*, 16 Sept. 1854.

VIII 17   Enbrook, near Folkestone. By S. S. Teulon, 1853–55. Plan from *Builder*, 16 Sept. 1854.

VIII 18   Aldermaston Court, near Newbury. By P. C. Hardwick, 1848–51. Photo. *Country Life.*

VIII 19   Peckforton Castle, near Bunbury, Cheshire. By Anthony Salvin, 1846–50. *Corps de logis* from drawing at R.I.B.A.

VIII 20   Peckforton Castle, near Bunbury, Cheshire. By Anthony Salvin, 1846–50. Distant view from watercolor at R.I.B.A.

VIII 21   Peckforton Castle, near Bunbury, Cheshire. Anthony Salvin, 1846–50. View inside court from watercolor at R.I.B.A.

VIII 22   Lismore Castle, Waterford, Ireland. By Sir Joseph Paxton and G. H. Stokes, 1850–57. From *Building News*, 8 Jan. 1858.

VIII 23   Ruthin Castle, Ruthin, Denbigshire. By Henry Clutton, 1851–53. From *Builder*, 10 Sept. 1853.

VIII 24   Mentmore, near Cheddington, Buckinghamshire. By Sir Joseph Paxton and G. H. Stokes, 1852–54. From *Builder*, 10 Dec. 1857.

VIII 25   Balmoral Castle III, near Ballater, Fifeshire. By William Smith of Aberdeen and Prince Albert, 1853–55. Entrance front. Photo. *Picture Post.*

VIII 26   Balmoral Castle I, near Ballater, Fifeshire. By William Smith of Aberdeen, c.1845. From *Illustrated London News*, 1 Sept. 1849.

VIII 27   Balmoral Castle III, near Ballater, Fifeshire. By William Smith of Aberdeen and Prince Albert, 1853–55. Garden front. Photo. *Picture Post.*

VIII 28   Balmoral Castle III, near Ballater, Fifeshire. By William Smith of Aberdeen and Prince Albert, 1853–55. Distant view. Photo. *Picture Post.*

VIII 29   Buchanan House, near Glasgow. By William Burn, 1851–54. Perspective, dated 16 Jan. 1852, and plan, dated Mar. 1853, from drawings at R.I.B.A.

VIII 30   Project for Fonthill House, near Hinton, Wiltshire. By William Burn, c.1847. From watercolor at R.I.B.A.

VIII 31   Fonthill House, near Hinton, Wiltshire. By William Burn, c.1847–52. Photo. *Country Life.*

VIII 32   Clonghanadfoy Castle, near Limerick, Ireland. By G. F. Jones of York, c.1848–50. From *Builder*, 23 Nov. 1850.

VIII 33   Balentore, Scotland. By William Burn, c.1850. From watercolor at R.I.B.A.

VIII 34   Bylaugh Hall, near East Dereham, Norfolk. By Banks and Barry, 1849–52. From *Building News*, 26 Mar. 1869.

VIII 35   Grittleton House, near Chippenham, Wiltshire. By James Thomson, c.1845–60. From *Builder*, 30 Apr. 1853.

X 1   The Royal Exchange, London. By Sir William Tite, (1839) 1840–44. West front from *Architect, Engineer and Surveyor*, 1840.

X 2   The Royal Exchange, London. By Sir William Tite, (1839) 1841–44. South front from *Illustrated London News*, 26 Oct. 1844.

X 3   The Royal Exchange, London. By Sir William Tite, (1839) 1841–44. Court, with Royal procession at opening, from *Illustrated London News*, 2 Nov. 1844.

X 4   The Royal Exchange, London. By Sir William Tite, (1839) 1841–44. South and east fronts from *Illustrated London News*, 26 Oct. 1844.

X 5   Fitzwilliam Museum, Trumpington St., Cambridge. By George Basevi and C. R. Cockerell, 1837–47. Photo. *Picture Post*.

X 6   St. George's Hall, Lime St., Liverpool. By H. L. Elmes, Sir Robert Rawlinson, and C. R. Cockerell, (1839–40) 1841–47, 1847–49, 1851–54 (1856). East front. Photo. *Picture Post*.

X 7   St. George's Hall, Lime St., Liverpool. By H. L. Elmes, Robert Rawlinson, and C. R. Cockerell, (1839–40) 1841–47, 1847–49, 1851–54 (1856). Plan from *Builder*, 6 Jan. 1855.

X 8   St. George's Hall, Lime St., Liverpool. By H. L. Elmes, Robert Rawlinson, and C. R. Cockerell, (1839–40) 1841–47, 1847–49, 1851–54 (1856). North end. Photo. N.B.R.

X 9   University Galleries and Taylor Institute (Ashmolean), Beaumont and St. Giles Sts., Oxford. By C. R. Cockerell, (1840) 1841–45. Elevation toward Beaumont St. from *Builder*, 24 Oct. 1846.

X 10 University Galleries and Taylor Institute (Ashmolean), Beaumont and St. Giles Sts., Oxford. By C. R. Cockerell, (1840) 1841–45. Plan from *Builder*, 24 Oct. 1846.

X 11 University Galleries and Taylor Institute (Ashmolean), Beaumont and St. Giles Sts., Oxford. By C. R. Cockerell, (1840) 1841–45. East front from A. E. Richardson, *Monumental Classic Architecture* [1914].

X 12 Hall and Library of Lincoln's Inn, London. By Philip and P. C. Hardwick, 1843–45. West front toward Lincoln's Inn Fields from *Illustrated London News*, 1 Nov. 1845.

X 13 Hall and Library of Lincoln's Inn, London. By Philip and P. C. Hardwick, 1843–45. Plan from *Illustrated London News*, 1 Nov. 1845.

X 14 Coal Exchange, Lower Thames St., London. By J. B. Bunning, 1846–49. Court from *Builder*, 29 Sept. 1849.

X 15 Coal Exchange, Lower Thames St., London. By J. B. Bunning, 1846–49. From southeast. Photo. N.B.R.

X 16 Coal Exchange, Lower Thames St., London. By J. B. Bunning, 1846–49. Perspective from drawing at R.I.B.A.

X 17 Coal Exchange, Lower Thames St., London. By J. B. Bunning, 1846–49. Dome panels of tree-ferns designed by Melhado and executed by Sang. Photo. Helmut Gernsheim.

cis Thompson, 1845–50. Details of central pier from Edwin Clark, *The Britannia and Conway Tubular Bridges*, 1850.

48

don (Paddington II). By I. K. Brunel and M. D. Wyatt, 1852–54. Sheds from *Illustrated London News*, 8 July 1854.

XVI 37   Great Western Railway Station, Eastbourne Terrace, Paddington, London (Paddington II). By I. K. Brunel and M. D. Wyatt, 1852–54. Interior wall of station block. Photo. R. H. de Burgh-Galwey.

XVI 38   "The Railway Station." By William P. Frith, 1861. From replica at Paddington Station.

XVI 39   Great Western Railway Station, Eastbourne Terrace, Paddington, London (Paddington II). By I. K. Brunel and M. D. Wyatt, 1852–54. Stationmaster's oriel. Photo. R. H. de Burgh-Galwey.

XVI 40   British Museum, Great Russell St., Bloomsbury, London. Reading Room by Sydney Smirke in construction, (1852) 1854–57. From *Illustrated London News*, 14 Apr. 1855.

XVI 41   Reading Room, British Museum, Great Russell St., Bloomsbury, London. By Sydney Smirke, (1852) 1854–57.

XVI 42   "The Aerial Ballet of the Brompton Boilermakers." (Museum of Science and Art, Brompton Park, London, by Young and Son, in construction, 1855–56.) Photo. Victoria and Albert Museum.

XVI 43   Museum of Science and Art, Brompton Park, London. By Young and Son, 1855–56. Sidewalls in construction. Photo. Victoria and Albert Museum.

XVI 44   Museum of Science and Art, Brompton Park, London. By Young and Son, 1855–56. Roof in construction. Photo. Victoria and Albert Museum.

XVI 45   Museum of Science and Art, Brompton Park, London. By Young and Son, 1855–56. Interior galleries before completion. Photo. Victoria and Albert Museum.

XVI 46   Museum of Science and Art, Brompton Park, London. By Young and Son, 1855–56. Interior at official opening from *Illustrated London News*, 12 Apr. 1856.

XVI 47   Museum of Science and Art, Brompton Park, London. By Young and Son, 1855–56. Entrance porch. Photo. Victoria and Albert Museum.

XVII 1   All Saints', Margaret St., Regent St., London. By William Butterfield, (1849) 1850–(1852)–1859. West front and tower. Photo. N.B.R.

XVII 2   All Saints', Margaret St., Regent St., London. By William Butterfield, (1849) 1850–(1852)–1859. First published view of exterior from *Builder*, 22 Jan. 1853.

XVII 3   All Saints', Margaret St., Regent St., London. By William Butterfield, (1849) 1850–(1852)–1859. South buttress with "Annunciation" relief. Photo. N.B.R.

XVII 4   All Saints', Margaret St., Regent St., London. By William Butterfield, (1849) 1850–(1852)–1859. Juxtaposition of south porch, tower shaft and choir school. Photo. N.B.R.

I THE STUDY OF VICTORIAN ARCHITECTURE

I 1 *Westminster New Palace, London. By Sir Charles Barry, A. N. W. Pugin, and E. M. Barry. Original design 1835–36; executed 1840–c.1865.*

I 2 *Athenaeum, Mosley St., Manchester. By Sir Charles Barry, 1837–39.*

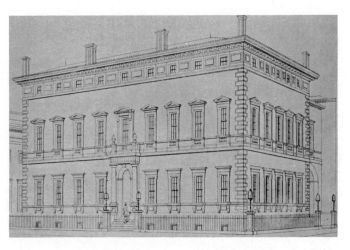

I 3 *Barry's original design for Athenaeum, 1836.*

I 4 St. Mary's, Southwark,
London. By Benjamin Ferrey,
1840–41.

I 5 St. Agatha's, Llanymynech,
Shropshire. By R. K. Penson,
1842–44.

I 6 Design for "Swiss Chalet."
By P. F. Robinson, 1827.

I 7   Highclere Castle, Hampshire.
By Sir Charles Barry, (1837) 1842–c.1855.

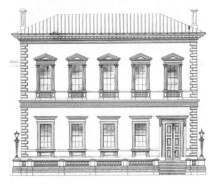

I 8   Travellers' Club House, Pall Mall, London.
By Sir Charles Barry, (1829) 1830–32.

I 9   Harlaxton Hall, Lincolnshire.
By Anthony Salvin, 1834–c.1855.
(Photo Country Life.)

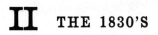

II THE 1830'S

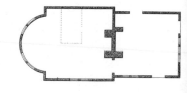

II 1   *"Pleasure Cottage." By James Malton, 1798. Exterior and plan.*

II 2   *"Rustic Double Cottage." By Sir John Soane, 1798. Exterior and plan.*

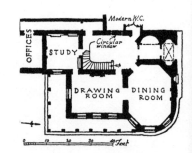

II 3   *Cronkhill, near Shrewsbury. By John Nash, c.1802. Exterior and plan.*

II 4 *"Four Cottages." By Joseph Gandy, 1805.*

II 5 *"Italian Villa." By Robert Lugar, 1805.*

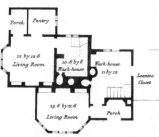

II 6 *"Double Cottage." By Robert Lugar, 1805. Elevation and plan.*

II 7 *Gwrych Castle,*
near Abergele,
Denbighshire, Wales.
By C. A. Busby and (?)
Lloyd Bamford Hesketh,
c.1814.

II 8 *Italian Villa.*
By J. B. Papworth, 1818.

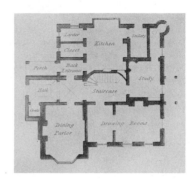

II 9 *"Vicarage House." By J. B. Papworth, 1818. Elevation and plan.*

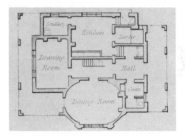

II 10 *"Cottage Ornée." By J. B. Papworth, 1818. Perspective and plan.*

II 11 *Lodge, Villa Borghese, Rome. From Charles Parker's* Villa rustica, *1832. Perspective and plan.*

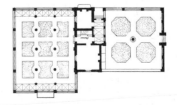

II 12 *"Gothic Villa." By E. B. Lamb, 1833.*

II 13 *"Gothic Villa." By E. B. Lamb, 1836.*

II 14 *"Italian Villa." By E. B. Lamb, 1836.*

II 15 *"Villa in the Cottage Style."*
By Francis Goodwin, c.1834.

II 16 *"Country Public House."*
By E. B. Lamb, 1833.

II 17 Royal Institution (now City Art Gallery), Manchester. By Sir Charles Barry, (1824) 1827–35.

II 18 St. Peter's Parish Church, Brighton.
By Sir Charles Barry, (1823) 1824–28.

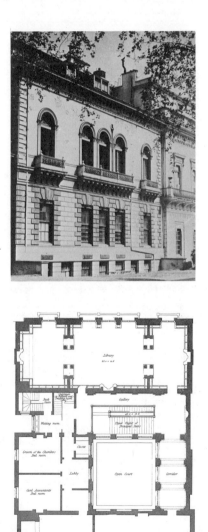

II 19 Travellers' Club House, London.
By Sir Charles Barry, (1829) 1830–32.
Garden front and plan.

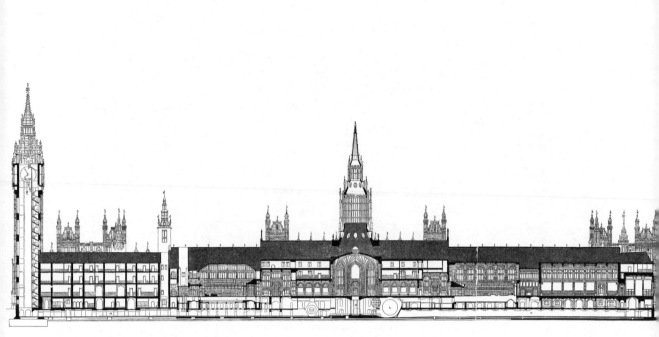

II 20   Westminster New Palace, London. By Sir Charles Barry and
A. N. W. Pugin, (1835–36) 1840–c.1865. Longitudinal section.

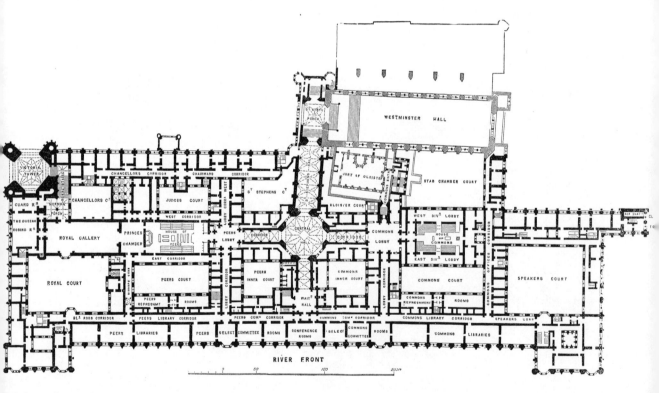

II 21   Plan of the principal floor.

II 22 Original design, south elevation.

II 23 Original design, north elevation.

II 24   Original design for Westminster New Palace, London.
By Sir Charles Barry and A. N. W. Pugin, c.1836. West elevation.

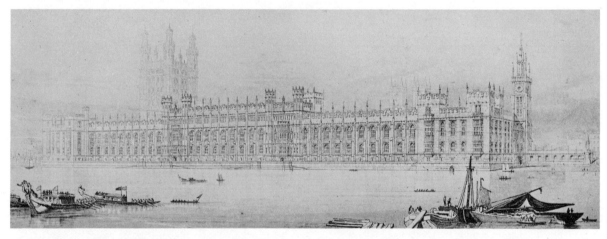

II 25   Perspective of river front as projected, 1836.

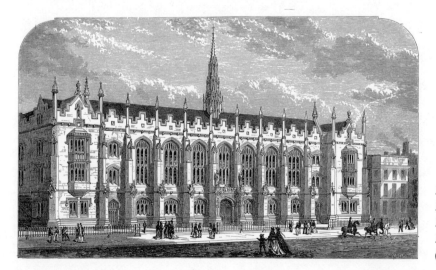

II 26   King Edward's
Free Grammar School,
New St., Birmingham.
By Sir Charles Barry,
(1833) 1834–37.

III PUGIN AS A CHURCH ARCHITECT

III 1 *Our Lady, Lisson Grove, London.*
By J. J. Scoles, 1833–34.

III 3 *Norman church.*
By G. E. Hamilton, 1836.

III 4 *St. Augustine's,*
Tunbridge Wells.
By Joseph Ireland, 1837–38.

III 2 *"Contrasted Public Inns," from*
A. N. W. Pugin's Contrasts, *1836.*

III 5 *St. Clement's, Oxford.*
Architect and date unknown.

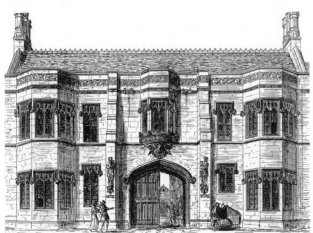

III 6   St. Marie's, Bridgegate, Derby.
By A. N. W. Pugin, 1838–39. West front.

III 7   Interior (painted decoration renewed 1930).

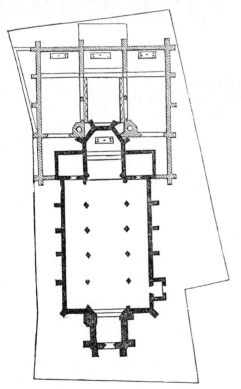

III 8   Plan, with indication
of projected eastward extension.

III 9   Nave arcade and clerestorey.

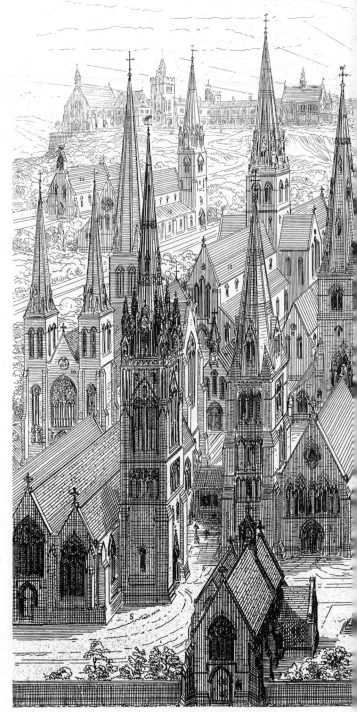

III 10   *The churches of A. N. W. Pugin,
from his* Apology for the Revival, 1843.

1. St. George's, Southwark, London
2. St. Peter's, Woolwich
3. St. Marie's, Stockton-on-Tees
4. St. Giles's, Cheadle
5. St. Marie's, Newcastle-on-Tyne
6. North Gate, St. Marie's, Oscott
7. St. Austin's, Kenilworth
8. Jesus Chapel, Pomfret
9. Cathedral, Killarney
10. St. Chad's, Birmingham
11. St. Oswald's,
    Old Swan, Liverpool
12. Holy Cross, Kirkham
13. St. Barnabas's, Nottingham
14. St. Michael Archangel's,
    Gorey, Ireland
15. St. Marie's, Derby
16. St. Alban's, Macclesfield
17. St. Marie's, Brewood
18. St. Winifride's, Shepshead
19. St. Andrew's, Cambridge
20. St. Bernard's Abbey, Coalville
21. St. Marie's, Keighley
22. St. Marie's, Warwick Bridge
23. St. Wilfrid's,
    Hulme, Manchester
24. St. Marie's, Southport
25. St. John's Hospital, Alton

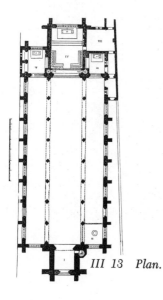

III 11   St. George's, Lambeth Rd., Southwark, London.
By A. N. W. Pugin, 1840–48. Interior after blitz.

III 12   Project for St. George's,
Southwark, 1838.

III 13   Plan.

III 14   Project for St. George's, Southwark. Interior.

III 15 Bishop Ryder's Church, Gem St., Birmingham. By Rickman and Hussey, 1837–38.

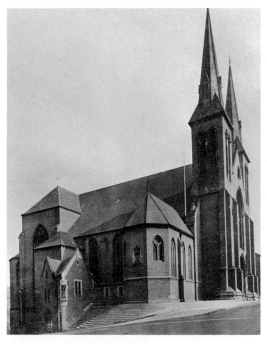

III 16 St. Chad's, Bath St., Birmingham. By A. N. W. Pugin, 1839–41. Exterior (with modern northwest chapel).

III 17 St. Chad's, Birmingham. Interior.

III 18 St. Chad's, Birmingham. West front.

III 19 St. Wilfrid's, Hulme, Manchester. By A. N. W. Pugin, 1839–42. Perspective and plan.

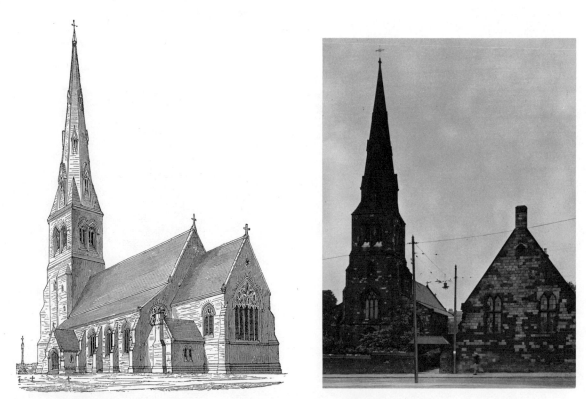

III 20 St. Oswald's, Old Swan, Liverpool. By A. N. W. Pugin, 1840–42.
Perspective from southeast and west front with school.

III 21 "Contrasted Residences of the Poor," from A. N. W. Pugin's Contrasts, *2d ed. 1841.*

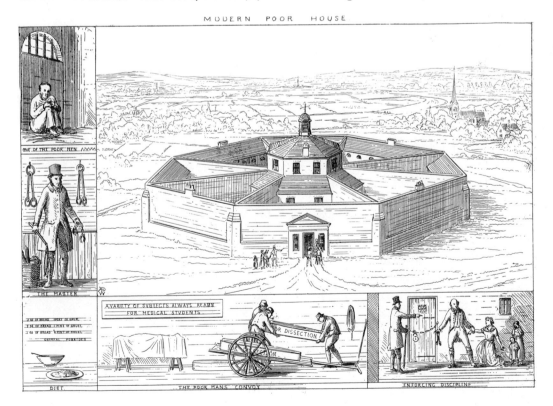

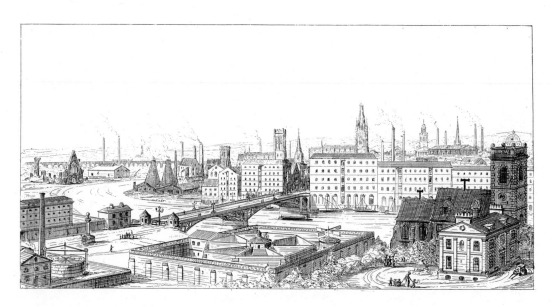

III 22 *"Contrasted English Towns, 1840 and 1440," from A. N. W. Pugin's* Contrasts, *2d ed. 1841.*

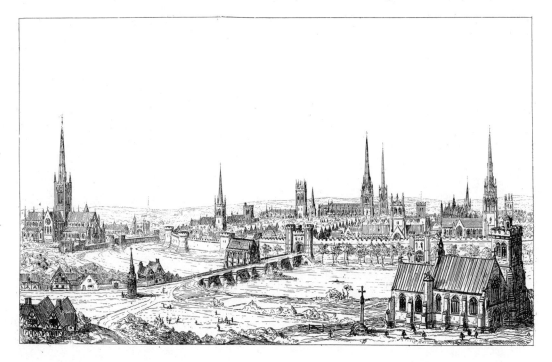

III 23   St. Mary's, Stockton-on-Tees, Co. Durham. By A. N. W. Pugin, 1840–42.

III 24   An ideal medieval parish church, from A. N. W. Pugin's True Principles, 1841.

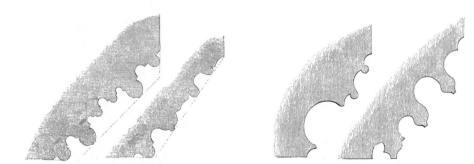

III 25   Approved and disapproved moldings, from A. N. W. Pugin's True Principles, 1841.

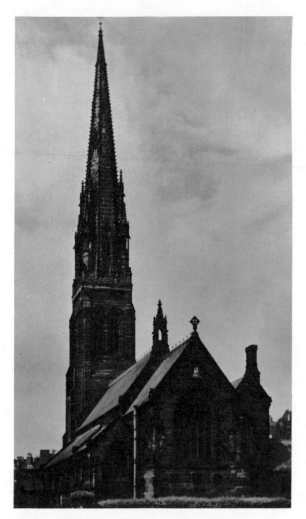

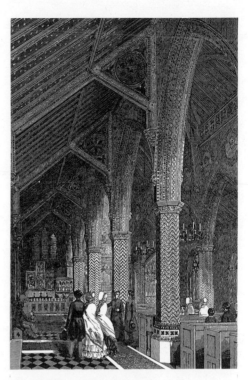

III 27   Interior.

III 26   St. Giles's, Cheadle, Staffordshire.
By A. N. W. Pugin, 1841–46.
Above, exterior from northeast; below, plan.

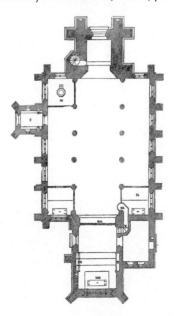

III 28   Interior, showing chancel screen.

III 29 St. Barnabas's, Derby Rd., Nottingham.
By A. N. W. Pugin, 1842–44.
Projected chancel decorations.

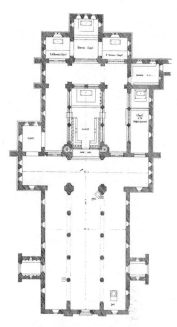

III 30 Plan.

III 31 Nave looking east.

III 32 Exterior from northeast.

III 33 Exterior from south.

III 34   St. Augustine's, West Cliff, Ramsgate, Kent.
By A. N. W. Pugin, 1846–51. Interior, looking east from south transept.

III 35   St. Augustine's. Exterior from southeast.

III 36   St. Augustine's. Floor tiles with Pugin's arms and monogram.

III 37   Our Lady of Victories, Clapham Park Rd.,
London. By W. W. Wardell, 1849–52.

III 40   Church of the Holy Apostles, Clifton Rd.,
Bristol. Interior, 1847–49. Architect unknown.

III 38   St. John's, White Cross
Bank, Salford. By Hadfield and
Weightman, 1844–48.

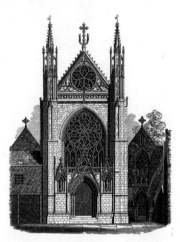

III 39   Immaculate Conception,
Farm St., Grosvenor Square,
London. By J. J. Scoles, 1844–49.

III 41   St. Raphael's, Kingston-
on-Thames, Surrey. By Charles
Parker, 1846–47.

IV ANGLICAN AND

NON-CONFORMIST CHURCHES

OF THE LATE 30'S AND

EARLY 40'S

IV 1   *Holy Trinity,*
Blackheath Hill, London.
By J. W. Wild, 1838–39.

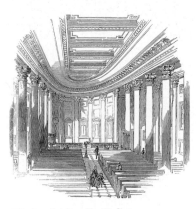

IV 2   *St. Paul's, Valetta,*
Malta. Begun 1839.

IV 3   *St. Laurence's, South-*
ampton. By J. W. Wild, 1839.

IV 4   *St. Peter's Parish Church, Kirkgate, Leeds.*
By R. D. Chantrell, 1839–41. Exterior from northeast.

IV 5   *Interior.*

IV 6 Ss. Mary and Nicholas's, Wilton, Wiltshire.
By Wyatt and Brandon, 1840–46. West front.

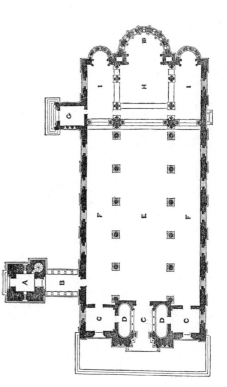

IV 7 Ss. Mary and Nicholas's. Plan.

IV 8 Ss. Mary and Nicholas's. Interior.

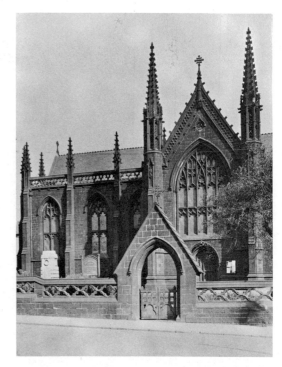

IV 9 Mill Hill Unitarian Chapel, Park Row,
Leeds. By Bowman and Crowther, 1847–48.

IV 10   *Christ Church, Streatham, London. By J. W. Wild, 1840–42.*

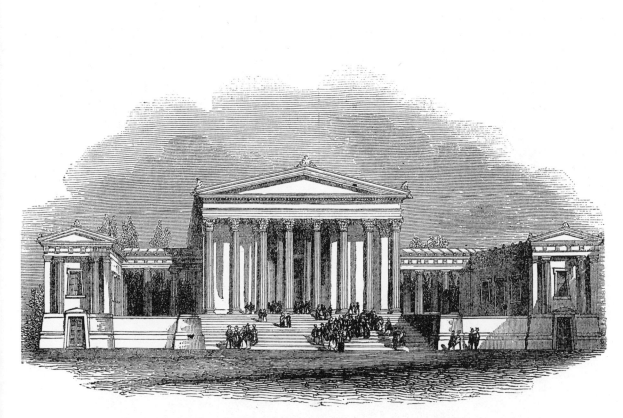

IV 11 *Great Thornton Street Chapel, Hull. By Lockwood and Allom, 1843.*

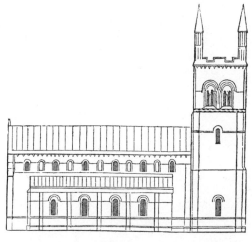

IV 12 *Church at Scofton, Nottinghamshire.*
By Ambrose Poynter, c.1840. From Charles
Anderson's Ancient Models, *new ed. 1841.*

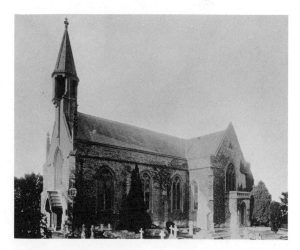

IV 13 *St. Matthew's,*
Otterbourne, Hampshire.
By W. C. Yonge, c.1840.

IV 14 St. Jude's, Manningham,
Bradford. By Walker Rawstone,
1841–43.

IV 15 St. Jude's, Old Bethnal Green
Rd., London. By Henry Clutton,
1844–46. Interior after blitz.

IV 16 All Saints' Parish Church, Leamington, Warwickshire.
By the Reverend John Craig, 1843–49.

IV 17   *St. Saviour's, Cavalier Hill, Leeds.*
By J. M. Derick, 1842–45.

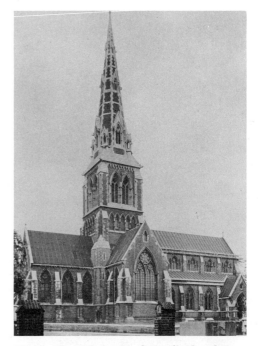

IV 19   *St. Giles's, Camberwell Church St.,*
London. By Scott and
Moffatt, 1842–44. Exterior from north.

IV 18   *Christ Church, Endell St., London.*
By Benjamin Ferrey, 1842–44.

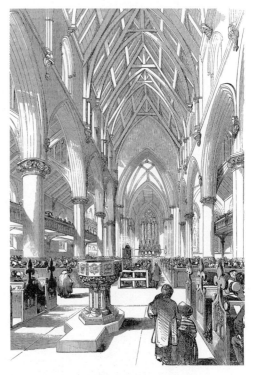

IV 20   *St. Giles's. Interior.*

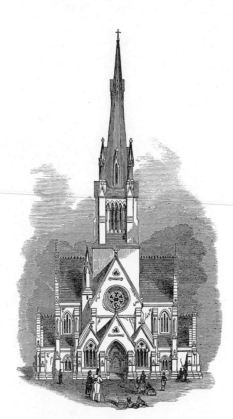

IV 21   Memorial Church, Colabah,
India. By J. M. Derick, c.1844.

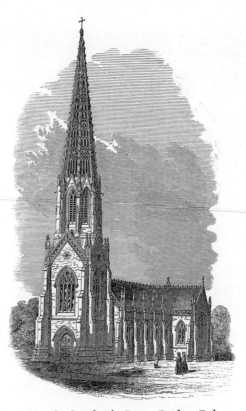

IV 22   St. Stephen's, Lever Bridge, Bolton-
le-Moors. By Edmund Sharpe, 1842–45.

IV 23   Holy Trinity, Gloucester Terrace,
Paddington, London.
By Thomas Cundy II, 1844–46.

IV 24   Martyrs' Memorial,
St. Giles St., Oxford.
By Sir G. G. Scott, 1841.

IV 25   *Holy Trinity, Rusholme, Manchester.*
By Edmund Sharpe, 1844–46.

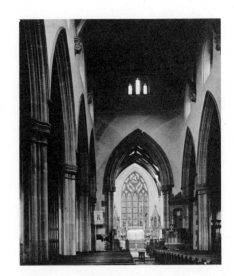

IV 26   *St. Alkmund's, Bridgegate, Derby.*
By I. H. Stevens, 1844–46.

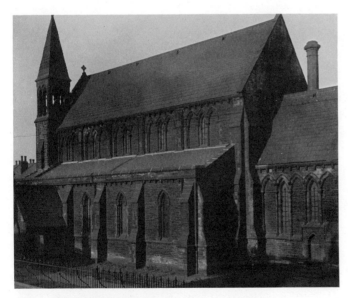

IV 27   *St. Andrew's, Leeds.*
By Scott and Moffatt, 1844–45.

IV 28   *St. Mark's, Swindon, Berkshire.*
By Scott and Moffatt, 1843–45.

IV 29 Walter Scott Monument, East Prince's St. Gardens, Edinburgh. By E. Meikle Kemp, (1836) 1840–46.

V ANGLICAN AND NON-CONFORMIST

CHURCHES OF THE LATE 40'S

V 1 *Clapham Congregational Church, Grafton Sq.,*
London. By John Tarring, 1850–52.

V 2 *Cavendish Street Independent Chapel,*
Manchester. By Edward Walters, 1847–48.

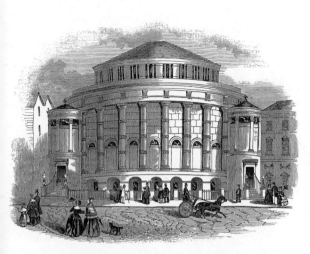

V 3 *Particular Baptist Chapel, Belvoir St.,*
Leicester. By J. A. Hansom, 1844–45.

V 4 *Central Baptist Chapel, Bloomsbury St.,*
London. By John Gibson, 1845–48.

V 5 *Accepted design for Nikolaikirche, Hamburg. By Sir G. G. Scott, (1844) 1845–63.*

V 6 *St. Andrew's, Wells St., London. By Dawkes and Hamilton, 1845–47.*

V 7 *St. Matthew's, City Road, London. By Sir G. G. Scott and (?) G. E. Street, 1847–48.*

V 8 *Independent Church, Glasgow. By J. T. Emmett, 1852.*

V 9   *St. Peter's, Tewksbury Rd., Cheltenham.*
By S. W. Dawkes, 1847–49. Exterior, from southeast.

V 10   *St. Peter's. Interior.*

V 11   *St. Ann's, New St., Alderney.*
By Sir G. G. Scott, 1847–50.

V 12   *St. Matthias's, Chilton St., London.*
By Wyatt and Brandon, 1847–48

V 13　St. Saviour's Vicarage, Coalpitheath, Gloucestershire. By William Butterfield, 1844–45.

V 14　Lychgate, St. Saviour's Churchyard, Coalpitheath, Gloucestershire. By William Butterfield, 1844–45.

V 15　Anglican Cathedral, St. John's, Newfoundland. By Sir G. G. Scott, begun 1846.

V 16 *Original design for St. Mary Magdalene's, Munster Sq., London. By R. C. Carpenter, 1849.*

V 17 *Interior.*

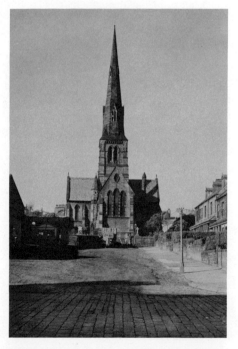

V 18 *St. Paul's, Manningham, Bradford. By Mallinson and Healey, 1847–48.*

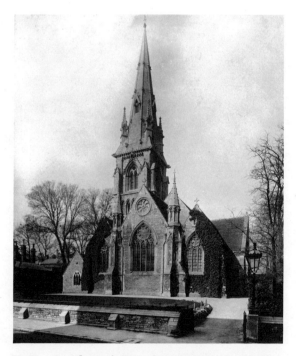

V 19 *St. Thomas's, Winchester. By E. W. Elmslie, (1844) 1845–46 (tower completed 1856–57).*

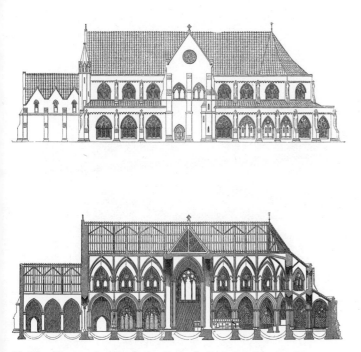

V 20 *Design for Anglican Cathedral, Colombo, Ceylon. By R. C. Carpenter, 1847. Side elevation and section.*

V 21 *Original design for St. Paul's, West St., Brighton. By R. C. Carpenter, 1846–48.*

V 22 *St. Paul's. Interior.*

V 23 *St. Paul's. East portal.*

V 24   St. John's College, Hurstpierpoint, Sussex. By R. C. Carpenter, 1851–53.

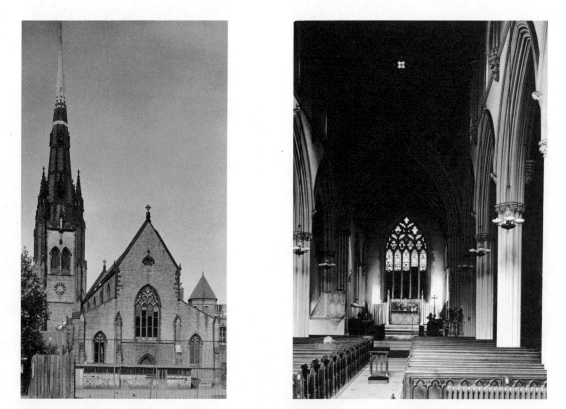

V 25   St. Stephen's, Rochester Row, London. By Benjamin Ferrey, 1847–50.   V 26   Interior.

V 27 St. Barnabas's, Pimlico,
London. By Thomas Cundy II and (?)
William Butterfield, 1846–50.

V 28 St. Barnabas's. Clergy House.

V 29 St. Barnabas's. Interior.

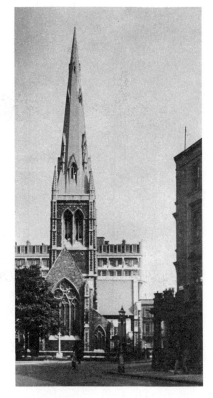

V 30 Holy Trinity, Bessborough
Gardens, London.
By J. L. Pearson, 1849–52.

V 31   Independent Chapel, Boston.
By Stephen Lewin, 1849–50.

V 33   St. Thomas's, Coventry. By Sharpe and Paley,
1848–49. Exterior, from northwest.

V 32   All Saints', Thirkleby,
Yorkshire. By E. B. Lamb. 1848–50.

V 34   Interior.

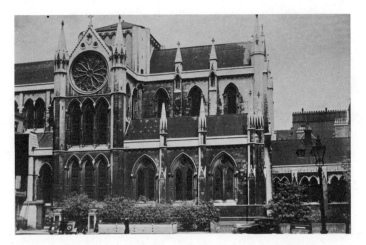

V 35 *Catholic Apostolic Church, Gordon Sq., London.*
By Brandon and Ritchie, 1850–54. Exterior from north.

V 36 *Interior.*

V 37   *Caledonia Rd. Free Church, Glasgow. By Alexander Thomson, 1856–57.*

VI BARRY AS AN ARCHITECT OF "PALACES"

VI 1   *Italian Gardens, Trentham Park, near Stoke-on-Trent. By Sir Charles Barry and W. A. Nesfield, c.1835–40.*

VI 2   *Trentham Park as altered by Sir Charles Barry, c.1835–c.1850. (Photo Country Life.)*

VI 3   *Town Hall, Crossley St., Halifax. By Sir Charles Barry and E. M. Barry, (1859) 1860–62.*

VI 4   Reform Club House, Pall Mall, London. By Sir Charles
Barry, (1837) 1838–40. Elevation.   VI 5   Plan.

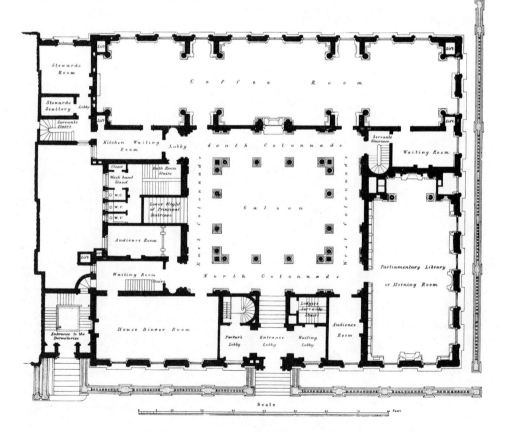

VI 6   *Reform Club House. North front, with Travellers' Club House beyond.*

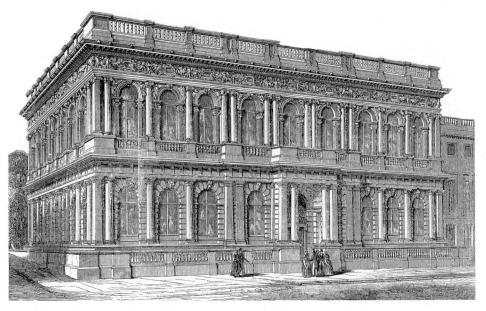

VI 7   *Carlton Club House, Pall Mall, London. Winning project by Sydney Smirke for new front, 1847.*

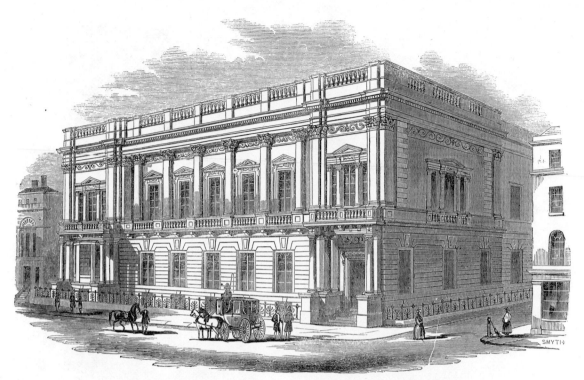

VI 8   *Conservative Club House, St. James's St., London. By George Basevi and Sydney Smirke, 1843–44.*

VI 9   *Army and Navy Club House, Pall Mall, London. By Parnell and Smith, 1848–51.*

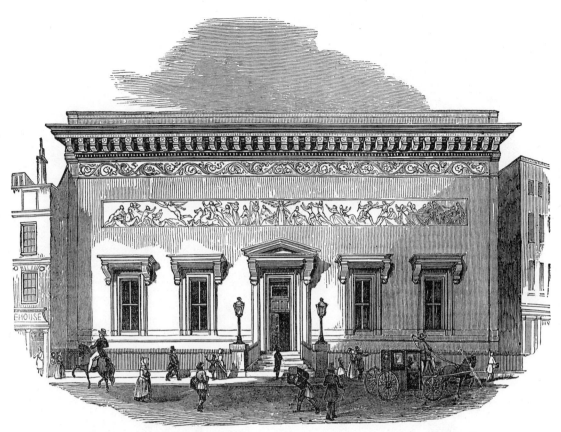

VI 10   Moxhay's Hall of Commerce, Threadneedle St., London, 1842–43.

VI 11   Hall of Physicians, Queen St.,
Edinburgh. By Thomas Hamilton, 1844–45.

VI 12   Southampton Yacht Club,
Southampton. By T. S. Hack, 1845.

VI 13 *Mansion, Kensington Palace Gardens, London. By J. T. Knowles, 1847.*

VI 16 *Plymouth and Cottonian Libraries, Plymouth. By George Wightwick, 1851–52. Front elevation.*

VI 17 *British Embassy, Constantinople. By Sir Charles Barry and W. J. Smith, (1842) 1845–47.*

VI 14 *Hudson Mansion, Albert Gate, London. By Thomas Cubitt, 1843–45. (Conservatory not original.)*

VI 15 *Athenaeum, Sheffield. By George Alexander, 1847–48.*

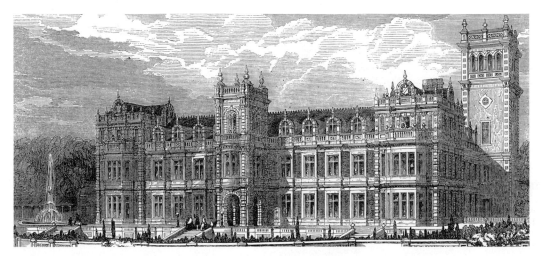

VI 18　*Somerleyton Hall, near Lowestoft. As refaced by John Thomas, 1844–51.*

VI 19　*Highclere Castle, near Burghclere, Hampshire. As refaced by Sir Charles Barry, (1837) 1842–44.*

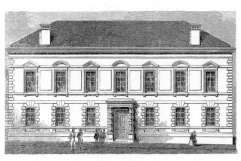

VI 20　*Athenaeum, Bury, Lancashire.*
By Sydney Smirke, 1850–51.

VI 21　*Mansion, Kensington Palace Gardens,*
London. By R. R. Banks, 1845.

VI 22   *Osborne House, near East Cowes, Isle of Wight. By Prince Albert and*
Thomas Cubitt. Private pavilion, 1845–46.   VI 23   *Garden front, 1847–49.*

VI 24   *Harlaxton Hall. By Anthony Salvin, 1834–c.1855. (Photo Country Life.)*

VII   THE BARRY STORY CONTINUED

VII 1   *City of London Prison, Camden Rd., London. By J. B. Bunning, 1851–52.*

VII 2   *Pentonville Prison, London. By Sir Charles Barry, 1841–43. Plan.*   VII 3   *Entrance block.*

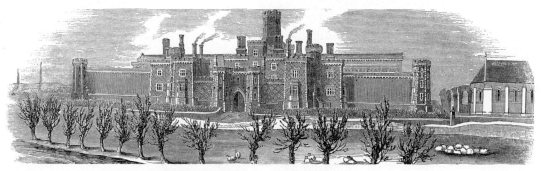

VII 4   *Berkshire County Gaol, Reading. By Scott and Moffatt, 1842–44.*

VII 5   *Dunrobin Castle, Sutherlandshire. By Sir Charles Barry and Leslie of Aberdeen, (1844) 1845–48.*

VII 6   *Board of Trade, Whitehall, London. By Sir Charles Barry, 1845–47.*

VII 7 *Bridgewater House, Cleveland Sq., London. By Sir Charles Barry, 1847–57. Entrance front.*

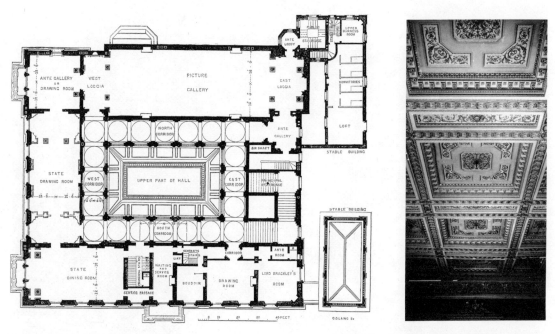

VII 8 *Bridgewater House. Plan.*

VII 9 *Ceiling in large drawing room.*

VII 10 *Bridgewater House. Green Park front.*

VII 11 *Bridgewater House. Doorcase in large drawing room.*

VII 12 *Picture Gallery after blitz.*

VII 13 *Dorchester House, Park Lane, London. By Lewis Vulliamy, 1848–63. Park front.*

VII 14 *Dorchester House. Plan.*

VII 15 *Dorchester House. Entrance court.*

VII 16   Great Western Hotel, Paddington, London. By P. C. Hardwick, 1851–53.

VII 17   Henry Thomas Hope House,
Piccadilly at Down St., London. By P. C. Dusillon
and T. L. Donaldson, 1848–51.

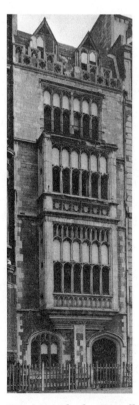

VII 18   Charles Russell
House, 23 Park Lane,
London. By W. B. Moffatt,
1846–48.

VII 19 *General Hospital,*
Bristol. By W. B. Gingell,
(1852) 1853–57.

VII 20 *Shrubland Park,*
near Ipswich. As remodeled by
Sir Charles Barry, 1848–50.

VII 21 *Cliveden, near*
Maidenhead. By Sir
Charles Barry, 1849–51.
(Photo Country Life.)

VIII MANORIAL AND

CASTELLATED COUNTRY HOUSES

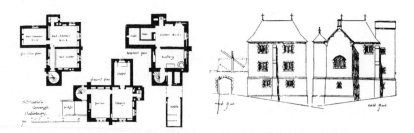

VIII 1   St. Marie's Grange, near Salisbury. By A. N. W. Pugin,
1835–36. Plans and elevations.

VIII 2   Project for additions to Scarisbrick Hall, Lancashire.
By A. N. W. Pugin, 1837.

VIII 3   Scarisbrick Hall, near Ormskirk, Lancashire.
As remodeled by A. N. W. Pugin, 1837–52, and E. W. Pugin, 1860–68.

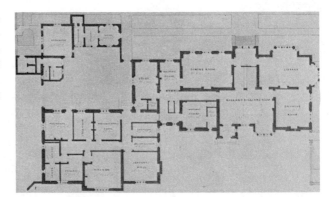

VIII 4 *Scotney Castle,*
Lamberthurst, Kent.
By Anthony Salvin, 1837–40.
Entrance front (above)
and plan (right).
(Photo Country Life.)

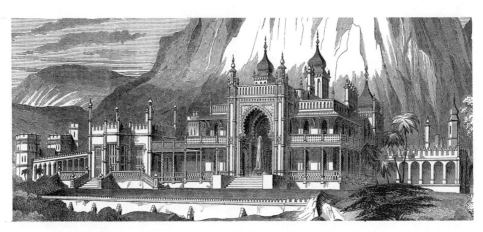

VIII 5 *Alupka, near Yalta, Crimea. By Edward Blore, 1837–40.*

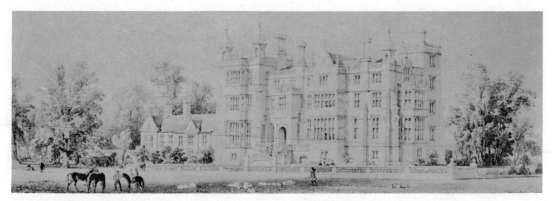

VIII 6   *Ramsey Abbey, Huntingdonshire. By Edward Blore, 1838–39.*

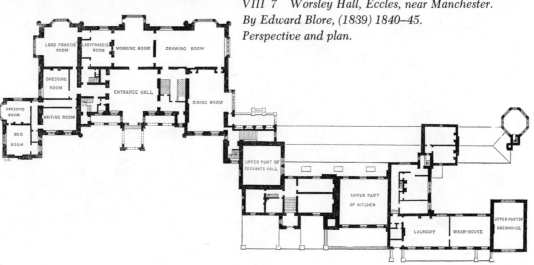

VIII 7   *Worsley Hall, Eccles, near Manchester.*
By Edward Blore, (1839) 1840–45.
Perspective and plan.

VIII 8 *Wray Castle, Lake Windermere.*
By Horner of Liverpool, 1840–47.

VIII 9 *Alton Castle, Staffordshire.*
Rebuilt by A. N. W. Pugin, c.1840.

VIII 10 *St. Marie's Presbytery, Bridgegate,*
Derby. By A. N. W. Pugin, c.1840.

VIII 11 *Convent of Sisters of Mercy, Hunter Rd.,*
Birmingham. By A. N. W. Pugin, 1840–41.

VIII 12   *Alton Towers, Staffordshire. Exterior of hall by A. N. W. Pugin, 1849.*

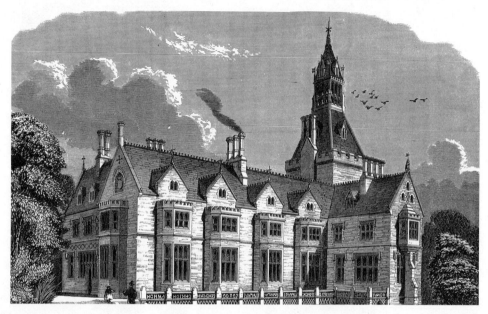

VIII 13   *Bilton Grange, near Rugby. By A. N. W. Pugin, 1841–46.*

VIII 14   *The Grange, West Cliff, Ramsgate. By A. N. W. Pugin, 1841–43.*

VIII 15   Tortworth Court, Cromhall, Gloucestershire. By S. S. Teulon, 1849–53. Perspective and plan.

VIII 16   Enbrook, near Folkestone. By S. S. Teulon, 1853–55.   VIII 17   Plan.

VIII 18   Aldermaston Court, near Newbury. By P. C. Hardwick, 1848–51. (Photo Country Life.)

VIII 19   *Peckforton Castle, Cheshire. By Anthony Salvin, 1846–50. Corps de logis.*

VIII 20   *Peckforton Castle.*

VIII 21   *Peckforton Castle. Inside the court.*

VIII 22   *Lismore Castle, near Waterford, Ireland. By Sir Joseph Paxton and G. H. Stokes, 1850–57.*

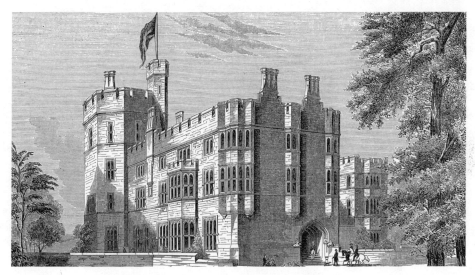

VIII 23   *Ruthin Castle, Denbighshire. By Henry Clutton, 1851–53.*

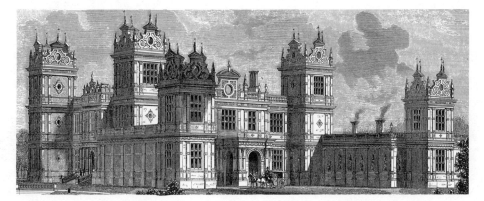

VIII 24   *Mentmore, near Cheddington, Buckinghamshire. By Sir Joseph Paxton and G. H. Stokes, 1852–54.*

VIII 26 *Balmoral Castle I.*
By William Smith, c.1845.

VIII 27 *Balmoral Castle III. Garden front.*

VIII 25 *Balmoral Castle III,*
near Ballater, Fifeshire.
By William Smith of Aberdeen
and Prince Albert, 1853–55.
The front entrance.

VIII 28 *Balmoral Castle III.*
Distant view.

VIII 29   Buchanan House, near Glasgow. By William Burn, 1851–54. Perspective and plan.

VIII 30   Project for Fonthill House, near Hinton, Wiltshire. By William Burn, c.1847–52.

VIII 31   Fonthill House, c.1847–52. (Photo Country Life.)

VIII 32 *Clonghanadfoy Castle, near Limerick, Ireland. By G. F. Jones of York, c.1848–50.*

VIII 33 *Balentore, Scotland. By William Burn, c.1850.*

VIII 34 *Bylaugh Hall,*
near East Dereham, Norfolk.
By Banks and Barry, 1849–52.

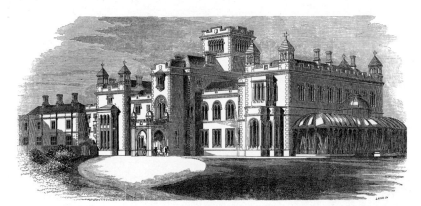

VIII 35 *Grittleton House,*
near Chippenham, Wiltshire.
By James Thomson, c.1845–60.

VIII 36 *Vinters, near*
Maidstone. As remodeled by
C. J. Richardson, 1850.

IX ROYAL AND STATE PATRONAGE

IX 1   *Buckingham Palace, London. East front by Edward Blore, 1846–48.*

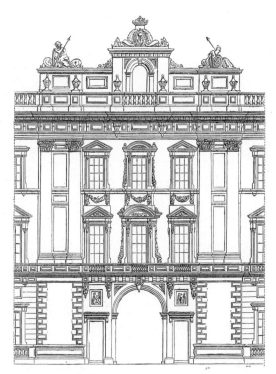

IX 2   *Central Pavilion.*

IX 3   *Chapel. By Edward Blore, 1842–43.*

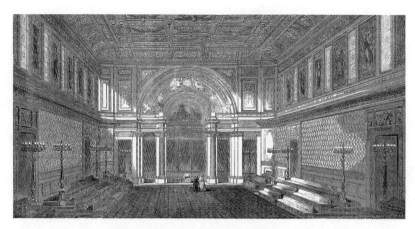

IX 4   *Ballroom. By Sir James Pennethorne, 1852–55.*

IX 5   *South wing. By Sir James Pennethorne, 1852–55.*

IX 6   *Supper Room. By Sir James Pennethorne, 1852–55.*

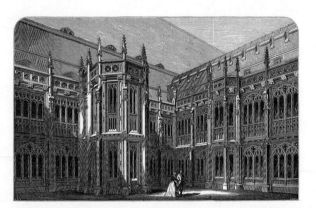

IX 7   *St. Stephen's Cloisters,
Westminster New Palace, London.
Built c.1526–29 but restored by
Sir Charles Barry and A. N. W. Pugin.*

IX 8   *Westminster New Palace, London. By Sir Charles Barry and A. N. W. Pugin.
The House of Lords, 1840–46.*

IX 9   *Peers' Lobby, 1840–46.*

IX 10   *Queen Victoria on throne in House of Lords receiving Speech from
Lord Chancellor at Opening of Parliament.*

IX 11   *Exterior of House of Lords, 1840–46.*

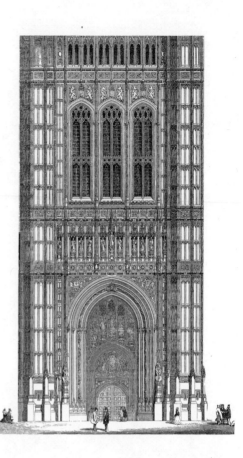

IX 12   *Westminster New Palace, London.*
Lower stages of Victoria Tower, 1840–52.

IX 13   *House of Commons. As first completed, 1840–49.*

IX 14   *House of Commons.*
As remodeled, 1850–51.

IX 15   *Victoria Lobby. 1840–46.*

IX 16   *Queen Victoria entering*
Royal Staircase.

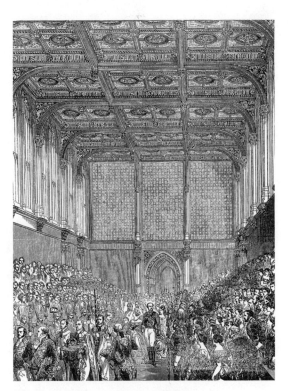

IX 17   *Victoria Gallery, with Queen*
Victoria approaching House of Lords.

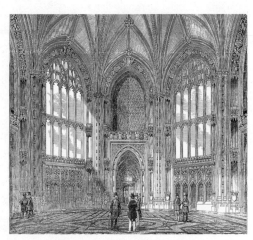

IX 18   Westminster New Palace.
Central Octagon.
(Before installation of mosaics.)

IX 19   St. Stephen's Hall.

IX 20   St. Stephen's Porch and portion of west front.
(Porch completed after Pugin's death in 1852 but before 1856.)

IX 21   *Westminster Hall, London.*
11th–14th centuries. St.
Stephen's Porch at the end by Sir
Charles Barry and A. N. W. Pugin.

IX 22   *Westminster New Palace.*
Library of House of
Lords. As completed, c.1852.

IX 23   *Westminster New Palace. Roofs seen from Victoria Tower,*
with lantern over Central Octagon in foreground and Clock Tower to rear.

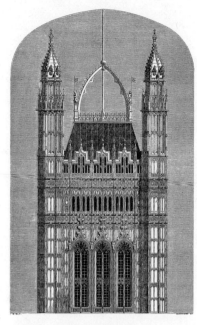

IX 24 *Westminster New Palace.*
Top of Victoria Tower as projected
by Barry before his death in 1860.

IX 25 *Westminster New Palace.*
By Sir Charles Barry and A. N. W. Pugin.
Belfry of Clock Tower in construction, 1857.

IX 26 *Museum of Economic Geology,*
London. By Sir James Pennethorne,
(c.1845) 1847–48 (1851). Jermyn St. entrance.

IX 27 *Museum of Economic Geology.*
Piccadilly front.

IX 28 *Museum of Economic Geology.*
Details of iron roof construction.

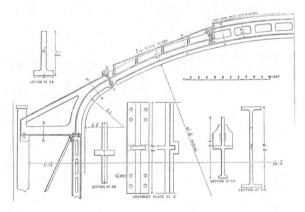

IX 29   *Museum of Economic Geology. Gallery.*

IX 30   *Record Office, Chancery Lane, London. By Sir James Pennethorne. The north front as projected, 1851.*

IX 31   *Ordnance Office, London. By Sir James Pennethorne, 1850–51. Pall Mall front.*

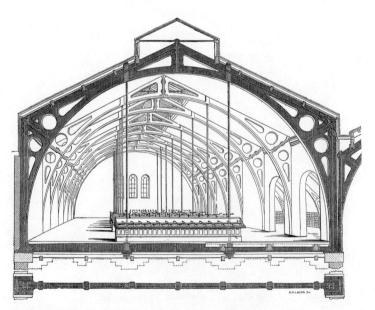

IX 32   *General Post Office, St. Martin-le-Grand, London. Sorting room added by Sydney Smirke, 1845.*

X CORPORATE ARCHITECTURE

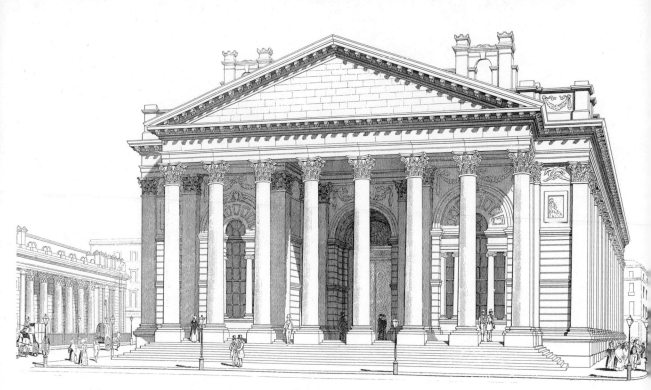

X 1   *The Royal Exchange, London. By Sir William Tite, (1839) 1840–44. West front.*

X 2   *South front.*

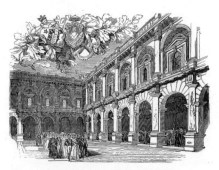

X 3   *The court, with Royal
procession at the opening.*

X 4   *South and east fronts.*

X 5   *Fitzwilliam Museum, Trumpington St., Cambridge. By George Basevi and C. R. Cockerell, 1837–47.*

X 6   *St. George's Hall, Lime St., Liverpool.*
By H. L. Elmes, Sir Robert Rawlinson, and C. R. Cockerell, (1839–40) 1841–54. East front.

X 7   *St. George's Hall. Plan.*   X 8   *North end.*

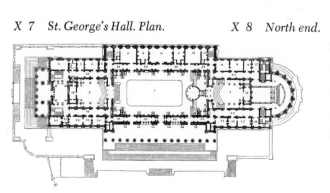

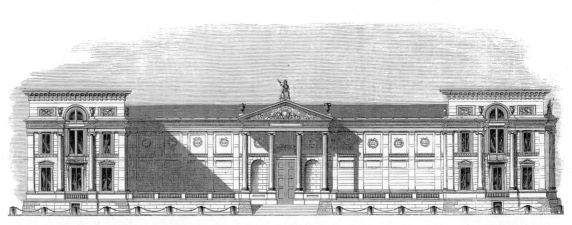

X 9   *University Galleries and Taylor Institute (Ashmolean), Beaumont and St. Giles Sts., Oxford.
By C. R. Cockerell, (1840) 1841–45. Elevation toward Beaumont St.*

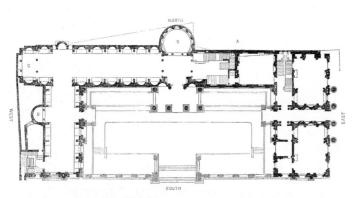

X 10   *University Galleries and Taylor Institute. Plan.*

X 11   *East front.*

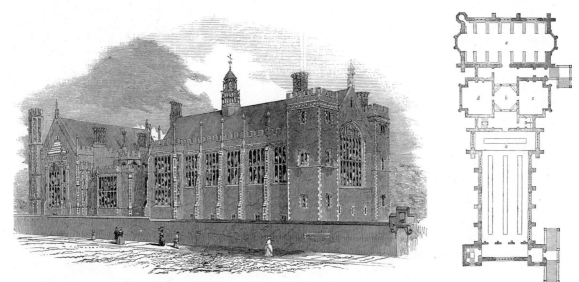

X 12   *Hall and Library of Lincoln's Inn, London. By Philip and
P. C. Hardwick, 1843–45. West front.*

X 13   *Plan.*

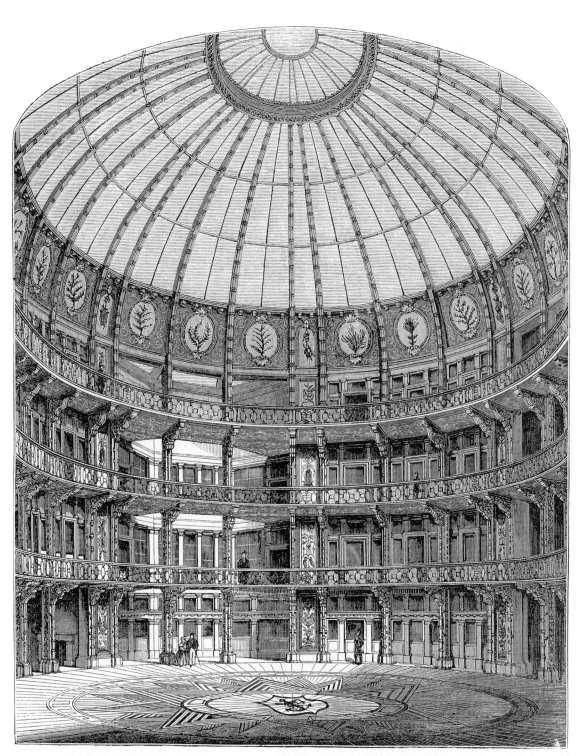

X 14   *Coal Exchange, Lower Thames St., London. By J. B. Bunning, 1846–49. The court.*

X 15   Coal Exchange. From the southeast.

X 16   Perspective.

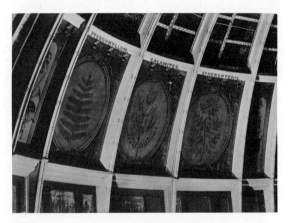

X 17   Dome panels of tree ferns
designed by Melhado and executed by Sang.

X 18   Colliery in panel
painted by Sang.

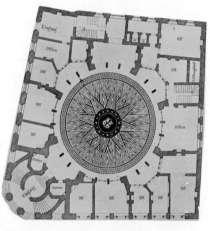

X 19   Plan.

X 20   "Jolly Miner" in panel
painted by Sang.

X 21   Coal Exchange. Dome ribs.

X 22   Second-storey stanchions.

X 23   Ground-storey stanchions.

X 24   First-storey stanchions.

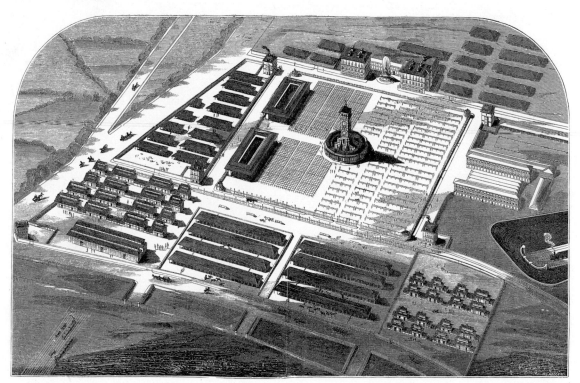

X 25   *Metropolitan Cattle Market*
(Caledonian Market), Copenhagen Fields, London. By J. B. Bunning, 1850–54.

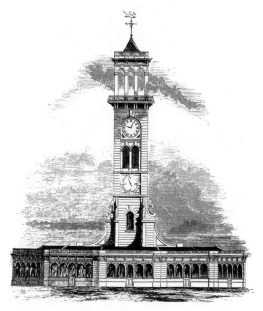

X 26   *Clock Tower and offices.*

X 27   *White Horse Tavern.*

X 28 Billingsgate Market, Lower Thames St., London. By J. B. Bunning, 1850–52.

X 29 Corn Exchange, Grass Market,
Edinburgh. By David Cousin, 1847–49.
Front and interior.

X 30 Town Hall and Market,
Truro, Cornwall. By Christopher
Eales, 1845–46. Front and rear.

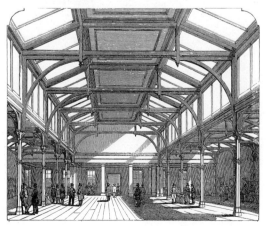

X 31 *Custom House, Ipswich.*
By J. M. Clark, 1843–45.

X 32 *St. Martin's Hall, Long Acre,*
London. By William Westmacott, 1847–50.

X 33 *Royal Academy Gold Medal project for a "Wellington College." By R. N. Shaw, 1853.*

X 34 *Wellington College, Sandhurst, Berkshire. Original design by John Shaw II, 1855.*

X 35   *Kneller Hall Training School, Whitton, Middlesex. By George Mair, 1848–50.*

X 36   *St. George's Hall, Bradford. By Lockwood and Mawson, 1851–53. Side and rear.*

X 37 St. George's Hall,
Lime St., Liverpool.
By H. L. Elmes, Robert Rawlinson,
and C. R. Cockerell,
(1839–40) 1841–47, 1847–49, 1851–54.
Opening of Great Hall.

X 38 Concert Room,
St. George's Hall.
By C. R. Cockerell, 1851–56.

X 39 *Concert Room, St. George's Hall. Stage.*

X 40   *National Gallery of Scotland, Edinburgh. By W. H. Playfair, 1850–54. (With the Royal Scottish Institution, 1822–36, on the right, and the Free Church College, 1846–50, behind; both also by Playfair.)*

X 41   *Royal Institution,*
Great Thornton St., Hull.
By Cuthbert Broderick,
1852–54.
Detail of entrance doorway.

XI BANKS AND INSURANCE BUILDINGS

XI 1   Bank Chambers, 3 Cook St., Liverpool. By C. R. Cockerell, 1849–50.

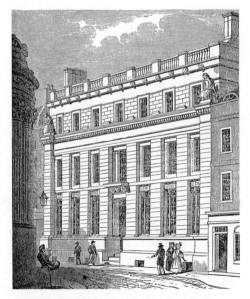

XI 2   London and Westminster Bank,
London. By C. R. Cockerell,
1837–38. Original façade.

XI 3   Legal and General Life Assurance
Office, London. By Thomas Hopper,
c.1838. (On the right.)
Center building by George Aitchison I, c.1855.

XI 4   Sun Fire and Life Assurance Offices, Bartholomew Lane and
Threadneedle St., London. By C. R. Cockerell, (1839) 1840–42.

XI 5   Liverpool and London Insurance
Offices, Dale St. and Exchange Pl.,
Liverpool. By C. R. Cockerell, 1856–58.

XI 6   Savings Bank, Bath.
By George Alexander, 1840–41.

XI 7   Commercial Bank of Scotland,
George St., Edinburgh.
By David Rhind, 1844–46.

XI 9   Branch Bank of England. Castle and Cook
Sts., Liverpool. By C. R. Cockerell, 1845–58.
Front and side.

XI 8   National Bank, Glasgow.
By John Gibson, 1847–49.

XI 10   Branch Bank of England, Broad St., Bristol. By C. R. Cockerell, 1844–46.

XI 11   *Stanley Dock, Liverpool. By Jesse Hartley, 1852–56. Warehouses after blitz.*

XI 12   *Royal Insurance Buildings,*
Liverpool. By William Grellier, 1846–49.

XI 13   *Stanley Dock.*
Walls and entrances.

XI 14   *Imperial Assurance Office,
London.
By John Gibson, 1846–48.*

XI 15   *Queen's Assurance and Commercial
Chambers, 42–44 Gresham St., London.
By Sancton Wood, 1851–52.*

XI 16   *Sir Benjamin Heywood's Bank, St. Ann's Sq., Manchester.
By J. E. Gregan, 1848–49. St. Ann's St. elevation (left) and entrance (right).*

XI 17   Corn Exchange (left) and Bank (right), Market Sq., Northampton.
By George Alexander and Hall, (1849) 1850–51, and E. F. Law, 1850, respectively.

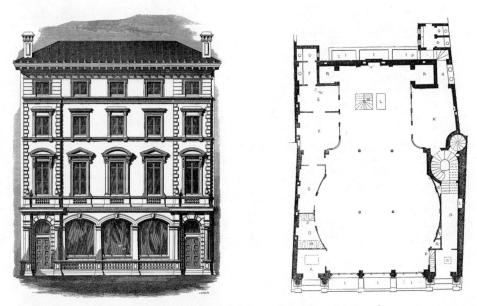

XI 18   London and Westminster Bank (Bloomsbury Branch), London.
By Henry Baker, 1853–54. Elevation and plan.

XII COMMERCIAL STREET ARCHITECTURE

XII 1 Brunswick Buildings, Liverpool.
By A. and G. Williams, 1841–42.

XII 2 Royal Exchange Buildings, Freeman's Pl., London. By Edward I'Anson and Son, 1844–45.

XII 3 Chambers,
Staple Inn, London.
By Wigg and Pownall,
1842–43.

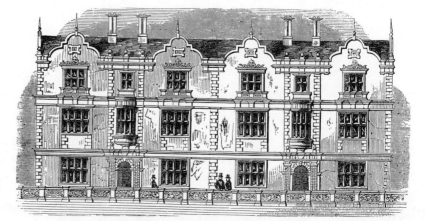

XII 4 Nos. 93–105
New Oxford St., London.
Possibly by Sir James
Pennethorne, c.1845–47.

XII 5 Faringdon St. North, London.
As intended to be completed, 1843.

XII 6 Block of shops, New Coventry St., London.
By Charles Mayhew, 1843–44.

XII 7 Nos. 44–50 New Oxford St.,
London. c.1845–47.

*XII 8   Nos. 75–77 New Oxford St., London.
Possibly by Sir James Pennethorne, c.1845–47.*

XII 9   Terrace of shops and houses, Queen St., Glasgow. By James Wylson, 1848.

*XII 10   Colonial Buildings,
Horse Fair and Windmill St.,
Birmingham. c.1845.*

XII 11   Nos. 5–9 Aldermanbury, London. c.1840?

XII 12   Boote Buildings,
Elliott St., Liverpool. 1846.

XII 13   No. 50 Watling St.,
London. c.1843?

XII 14   S. Schwabe Warehouse, 46–54 Mosley
St., Manchester. By Edward Walters, 1845.

XII 15   *The Quadrant, Regent St., London.*
By John Nash, 1819–20, but revised by Sir James Pennethorne, 1848.

XII 16   *James Brown, Son, and Co. Warehouse,*
9 Portland St., Manchester. By Edward Walters, 1851–52.

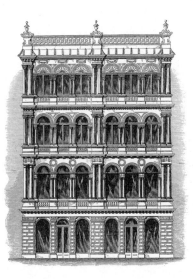

XII 17 *Two shops in Market St., Manchester.*
By Starkey and Cuffley, 1851.

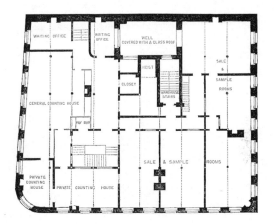

XII 18 *Warehouse, Portland and Parker Sts.,*
Manchester. By J. E. Gregan,
1850. Elevation and plan.

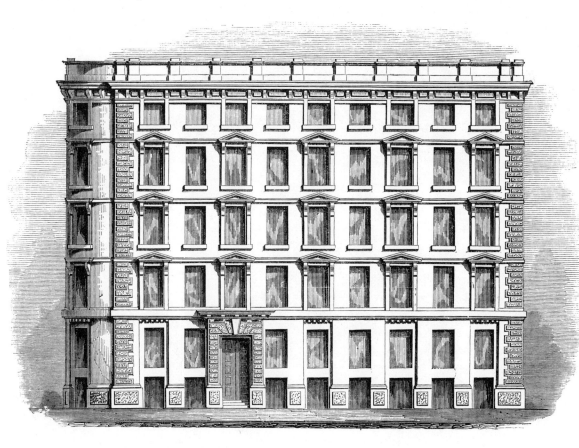

XII 19   *Shops and houses,*
New Oxford St., London.
By Henry Stansby, 1849.

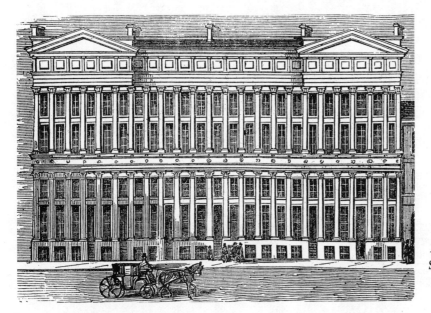

XII 20   *Warehouse in Mosley*
St., Manchester. Before 1851.

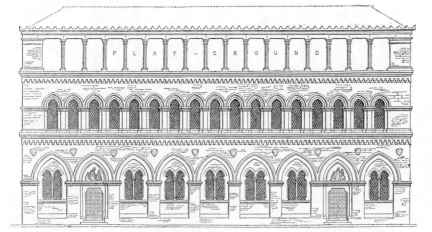

PLAY-GROUND

XII 21   *Northern Schools,*
St. Martin's-in-the-Fields,
Castle St., London.
By J. W. Wild, 1849–50.

XII 22 *Mr. Fair's shop and house, Prince's St., London, 1842.*

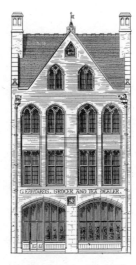

XII 23 *Project for grocer's shop. By A. N. W. Pugin, 1843.*

XII 24 *Perfumery shopfront, Piccadilly, London, 1850.*

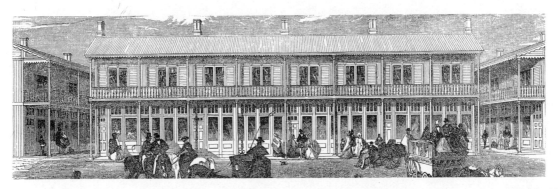

XII 25 *Prefabricated shops and dwellings, Melbourne, Australia. Made by Samuel Hemming in Bristol, 1853.*

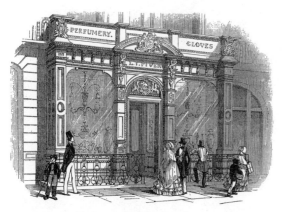

XII 26 *L. T. Piver shopfront, 160 Regent St., London. By Cambon, 1846.*

XII 27 *Shops in New Oxford St., London, 1851.*

XII 28   *Warehouse, 12 Temple St., Bristol. Perhaps by W. B. Gingell, c.1855.*

XII 29   *Nos. 188–192 Strand, London. By H. R. Abraham, 1852.*

XIII   THE BEGINNINGS OF VICTORIAN HOUSING

XIII 1   Gloucester Sq.,
from Hyde Park Sq.,
Bayswater, London.
1837–c.1847.
Northwest side
being demol-
ished in 1936.

XIII 2   Milner Sq.,
Islington, London.
By Gough and
Roumieu, 1841–43.
(Photo Country Life.)

XIII 3   Lonsdale Sq.,
Islington, London.
Begun by R. C.
Carpenter in 1838.
(Photo Country Life.)

XIII 4   Royal Promenade,
Victoria Sq., Clifton.
Begun 1837.

XIII 5   Worcester Terrace,
Clifton. Completed 1851–53
from earlier design.

XIII 6   Gloucester Sq., Bayswater,
London. Southeast side, c.1840–45.

XIII 7   Lansdowne Place, Plymouth.
Probably by George Wightwick, c.1845.

*XIII 8   Nos. 4–8
Eastgate St.,
Winchester. c.1840.*

*XIII 9   Nos. 10–20
Eastgate St.,
Winchester. c.1840.*

*XIII 10   Peacock Terrace,
Liverpool Grove,
Walworth, London. 1842.*

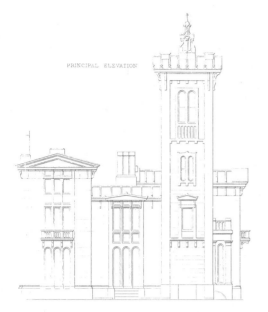

XIII 11 *"Grecian Villa."*
By S. H. Brooks, 1839.

XIII 12 *Semidetached "second-rate" houses.*
T. L. Walker's Architectural Precedents, *1841.*

XIII 13 *"Villa in the Florentine Style." By Richard Brown, 1842.*

Charles Parker Arch.t

Etched by J H Le Keux

XIII 14   *National School for 500 children. By Charles Parker, 1841.*

XIII 15   *"Villa in the Italian Style." By John White, 1845.*

XIII 16   Jacobethan entrance. By John White, 1845.

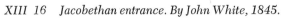

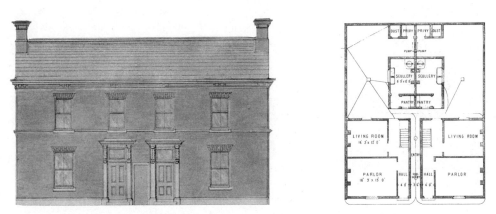

XIII 17   £200 row houses. By Samuel Hemming, c.1855. Elevation and plan.

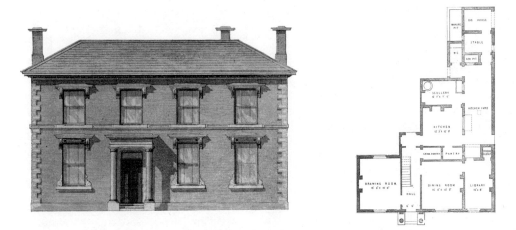

XIII 18   £670 parsonage house. By Samuel Hemming, c.1855. Elevation and plan.

XIII 19   Semidetached £750 houses. By Samuel Hemming, c.1855.

XIII 20   Terrace, Lowndes Sq., Belgravia, London. By Lewis Cubitt, 1841–43. Elevation and plans of corner house.

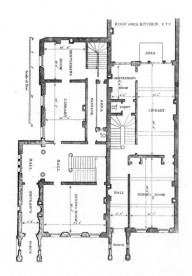

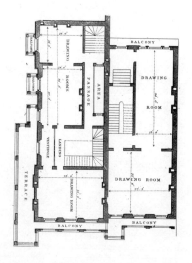

XIII 21 *Lyppiat Terrace, Cheltenham. Probably by R. W. Jearrad, c.1845.*

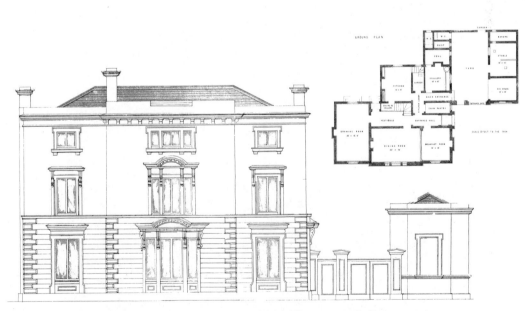

XIII 22 *£1550 villa. By Samuel Hemming, c.1855. Elevation and plan.*

XIII 23   *Terrace, Westbourne Terrace, Paddington, London. Probably by R. P. Browne, c.1845.*

XIII 24   *Westbourne Terrace. c.1845.*

XIII 25   *Quasi-semidetached houses, Westbourne Terrace. Probably by R. P. Browne, c.1845–50.*

XIII 26 *Gloucester Crescent, Camden Town, London. c.1850.*

XIII 27 *Kensington Gate, Gloucester Rd., London. Probably by Bean, c.1850.*

XIII 28 *Quasi-semidetached houses, Gloucester Terrace, Paddington, London. c.1845–50.*

*XIII 29 College Terrace,
Stepney, London.
c.1845–50.*

XIII 30 Llandudno, North Wales. By Wehnert and Ashdown (and others), 1849–55.

*XIII 31 St. Ann's
Villas, Norland Rd.,
London. c.1847.*

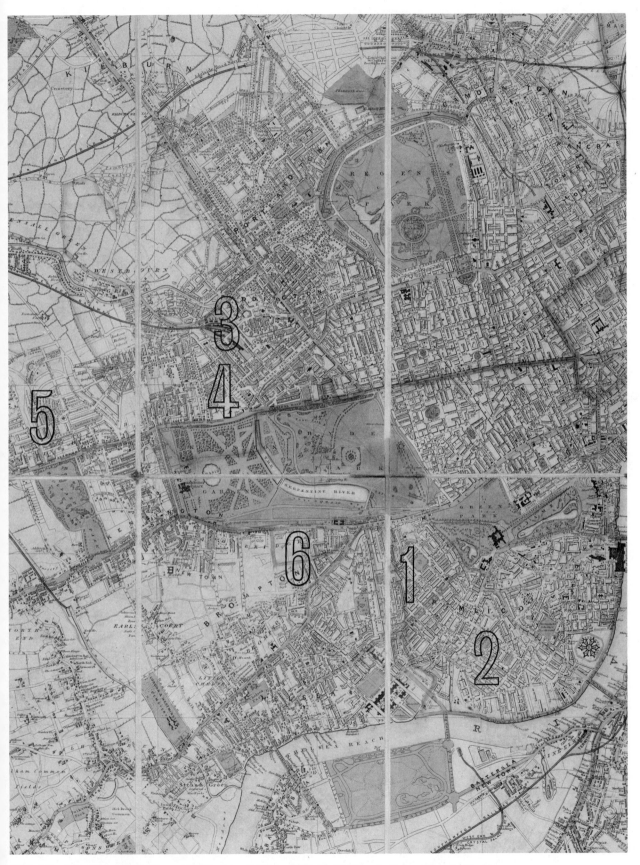

XIII 32   West London in the mid-50's. Map by James Wyld, 1858.   1. Belgravia   2. Pimlico
3. Paddington   4. Bayswater   5. Ladbroke Grove   6. Commissioners' Estate

XIII 33 *Blenheim Mount, Manningham Lane, Bradford. c.1855.*

XIII 34 *Terrace with shops below,*
St. George's Place, Knightsbridge, London. By F. R. Beeston, c.1848.

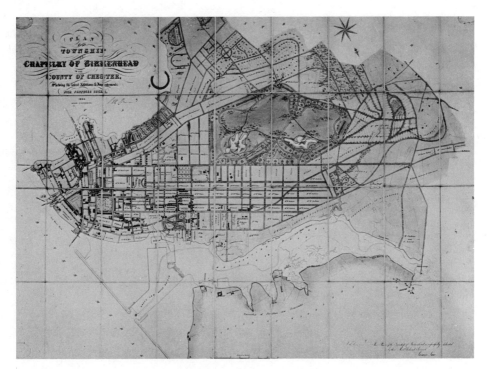

XIII 35   *Plan of Birkenhead in 1844, with proposed docks.*

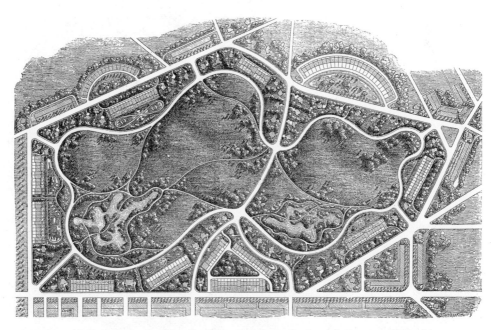

XIII 36   *Plan of Birkenhead Park, Birkenhead. By Sir Joseph Paxton, 1842–44.*

XIII 37 Semidetached houses,
39–41 White Ladies Road, Clifton. c.1855.

XIII 38 Birkenhead Park Lodge,
88 Park Rd. South, Birkenhead.
By Lewis Hornblower, 1844.

XIV HOUSING IN THE MID-CENTURY

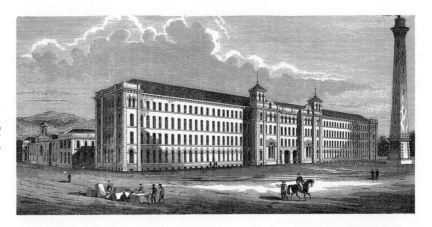

XIV 1 *Gloucester Arms
public house and contiguous
houses, Gloucester Terrace,
Paddington, London. c.1852.*

XIV 2 *Salt Mill,
Saltaire, near Bradford,
Yorkshire. By Lockwood
and Mawson, and Sir
William Fairbairn, 1851–53.
General view.*

XIV 3 *Salt Mill.
Entrance to offices.*

XIV 4 *Model Lodging House
for Single Men, George St.,
St. Giles, London.
By Henry Roberts, 1846–47.*

XIV 5 *Model Lodging Houses,
Clerkenwell, London.
By Henry Roberts, 1845–46.
Perspective and plans.*

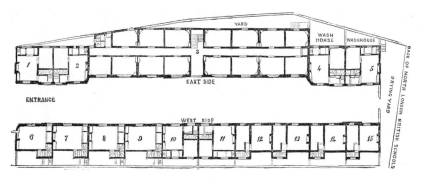

XIV 6   *Model Houses for Families (flatted),
Streatham and George Sts., Bloomsbury,
London. By Henry Roberts, 1849–50. Exterior.*

XIV 7   *Access galleries in court.*

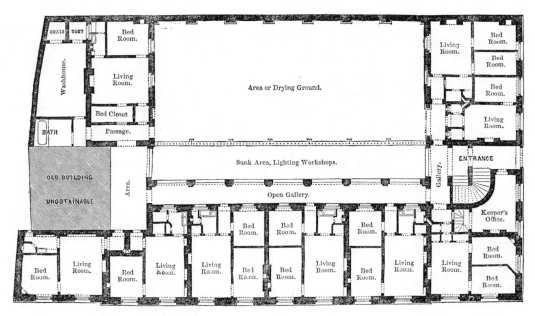

XIV 8   *Plan of ground floor.*

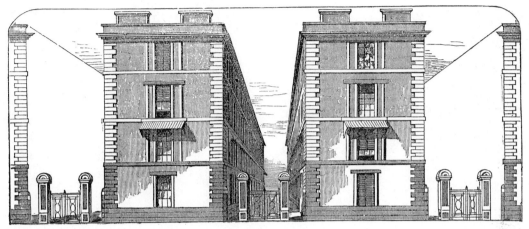

XIV 9   Workmen's Dwellings (flatted), Birkenhead. 1845–46.

XIV 10   Project for Model Town Houses for the Middle Classes (flatted). By William Young, 1849. Perspective and plans.

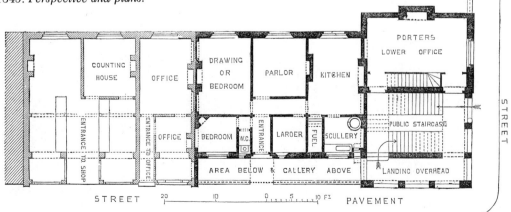

XIV 11 *Apartment houses in Victoria St. between Carlisle Pl. and Howick Pl. By Henry Ashton, 1852–54. General view looking east.*

XIV 12 *Typical upper-floor plan of one "house" with two apartments opening on one stair.*

XIV 13 *Terrace, Woodhouse Sq., Leeds. c.1850–55.*

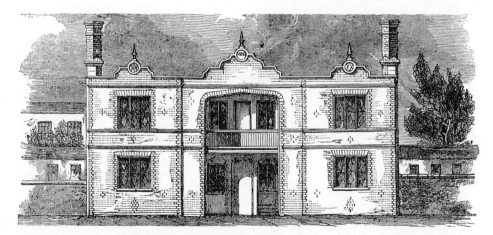

XIV 14 *Prince Albert's Model Houses, Hyde Park, London (now in Kennington Park). By Henry Roberts, 1850–51.*

XIV 15 *Prince's Gate, Kensington Rd., London. By Johnston, 1850–51. Front and rear elevations.*

XIV 16 *Nos. 70–74 Eastgate St., Winchester. c.1850.*

XIV 17 *St. Aidan's Terrace, Forest Rd., Birkenhead. Possibly by T. H. Wyatt, c.1853.*

XIV 18 South side of Grosvenor Sq.,
London. Three houses have Early
Victorian fronts, all probably
by Thomas Cundy II, c.1855.

XIV 19 Terrace, Hyde Park Sq.,
Bayswater, London. c.1840.

XIV 20 Terrace between Cleveland S
and Cleveland Gardens, Paddington,
London. c.1850–55. Entrance front.

XIV 21 Terrace, Moray Place, Strathbungo, Glasgow. By Alexander Thomson, 1860.

XIV 22 Terrace between Cleveland Sq.
and Cleveland Gardens, Paddington,
London. c.1850–55. Garden front.

XIV 23 Terrace,
Victoria Sq., Clifton.
c.1855.

XIV 24 *Walmer Crescent,*
Paisley Rd., Glasgow.
By Alexander Thomson, 1858.

XIV 25 *Queen's Park Terrace*
(flatted), Eglinton Street,
Glasgow. By Alexander Thomson,
1859.

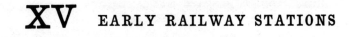

XV EARLY RAILWAY STATIONS

AND OTHER IRON CONSTRUCTION

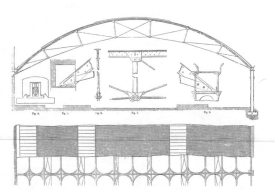

XV 1   Lime St. I Railway Station, Liverpool.
By John Cunningham, opened in 1836. Shed.

XV 2   Lime St. II Railway Station. Shed by
Richard Turner, 1849–51. Plan and section.

XV 3   Lime St. I Railway Station, Liverpool. Entrance Screen by John Foster, completed 1836.

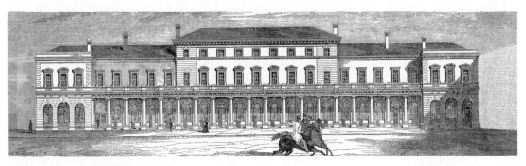

XV 4   Lime St. II Railway Station, Liverpool. Station block facing Lord Nelson St.
by Sir William Tite, 1846–50. Elevation.   XV 5   Plan.

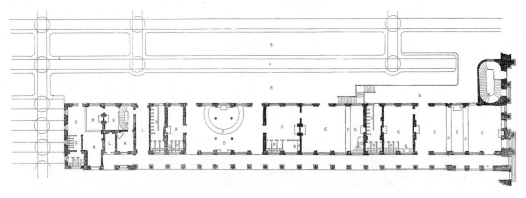

XV 6   Euston I Railway Station, London. The "Arch" by Philip Hardwick, 1835–37.

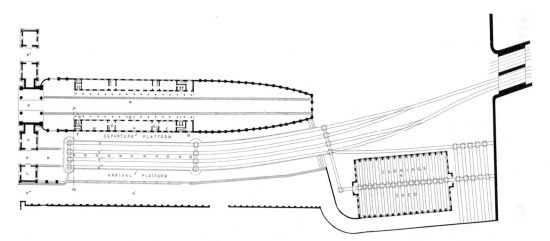

XV 7   Plan of Euston I Railway Station. By Robert Stephenson and Philip Hardwick, 1835–39.

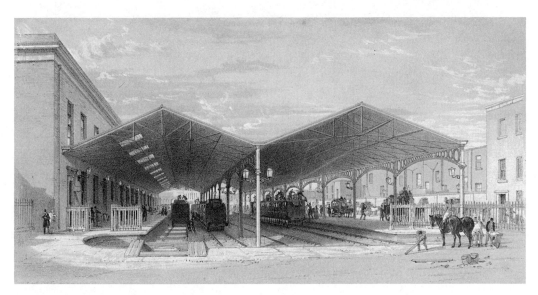

XV 8   Original departure and arrival sheds. By Robert Stephenson, 1835–39.

XV 9 *Projects for bridges on the "Antient Principles," with stations. By A. N. W. Pugin, 1843.*

XV 10 *Nine Elms Railway Station (now Transport Museum),*
Vauxhall, London. By Joseph Locke and Sir William Tite, 1837–38.

XV 11   Trijunct Railway Station and North Midland Station Hotel, Derby.
By Robert Stephenson and Francis Thompson, 1839–41.

XV 12   Trijunct Railway Station, Derby. Sheds.

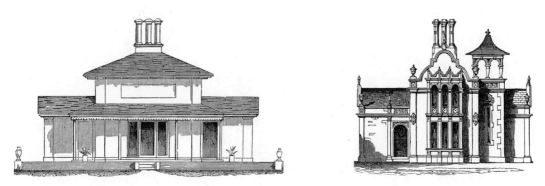

XV 13 and 14   Railway stations at Wingfield and Ambergate, Derbyshire. By Francis Thompson,
c.1840. "Revised to serve as cottage residences," by J. C. Loudon, 1842.

XV 15   Paddington I Railway Station, under Bishop's Rd., London. By I. K. Brunel, 1838.

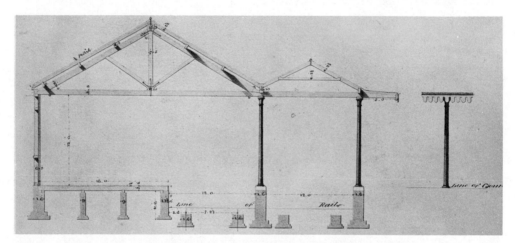

XV 16   Paddington I Railway Station, London. Section of shed.

XV 17   Clifton Suspension Bridge, Clifton Gorge.
Designed and begun by I. K. Brunel, and finished by W. H. Barlow, (1829) 1837–63.

XV 18 *The Queen's Hotel, Cheltenham.*
By R. W. Jearrad, opened in 1837.

XV 19 *Great Western Hotel,*
Bristol. By R. S. Pope, opened in 1839.

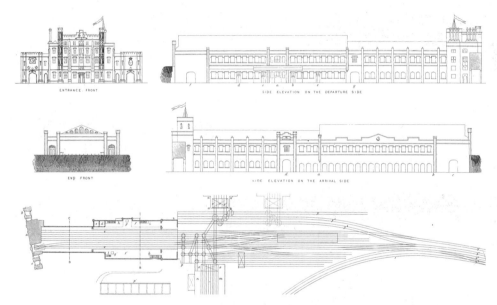

ENTRANCE FRONT

SIDE ELEVATION ON THE DEPARTURE SIDE

END FRONT

SIDE ELEVATION ON THE ARRIVAL SIDE

XV 20 *Temple Mead I Railway Station, Bristol. By I. K. Brunel, 1839–40. Plan and elevations.*

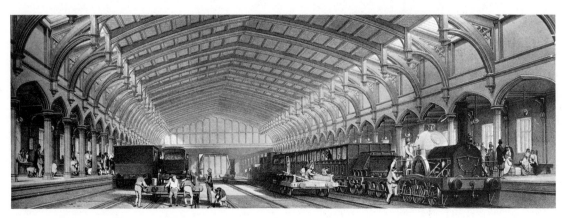

XV 21 *Temple Mead I Railway Station, Bristol. The shed.*

XV 22 *Great Northern Railway Station,*
Tanner Row, York. By T. G. Andrews, 1840–42. The triple shed, with the Queen entraining.

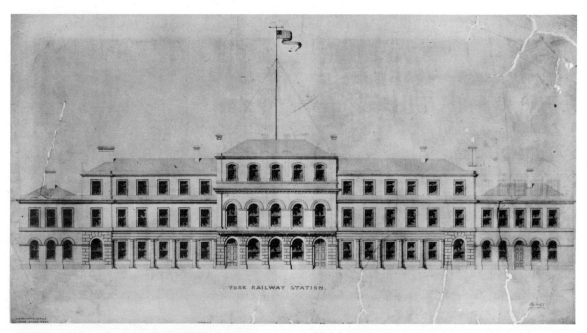

XV 23 *Great Northern Railway Station, York.*
Departure-side elevation, with added storey for hotel accommodation indicated over head-block to right.

XV 24 *South-Eastern Railway Station, Bricklayers' Arms,*
Southwark, London. By Lewis Cubitt, 1842–44. Entrance screen.

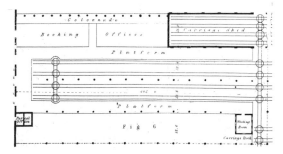

XV 25 *South-Eastern Railway Station,*
Bricklayers' Arms. Plan.

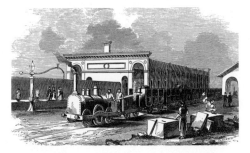

XV 26 *Eastern Counties Railway Station,*
Cambridge. By Sancton Wood, 1844–45.

XV 27 *Congleton Viaduct, North Staffordshire*
Railway. By J. C. Forsyth, opened in 1849.

XV 28 *Croydon and Epsom Atmospheric Railway*
Station, Epsom. By J. R. and J. A. Brandon, 1844–45.

XV 29 *Great Conservatory, Chatsworth. By Sir Joseph Paxton and Decimus Burton, (1836) 1837–40. (Photo Country L*

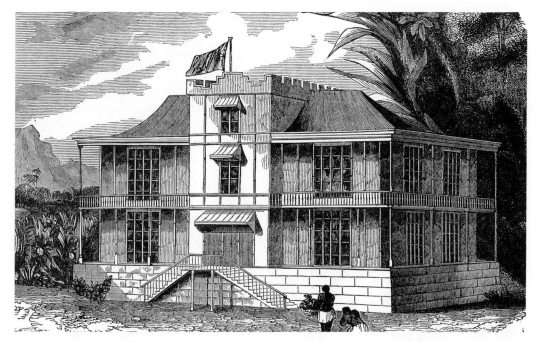

XV 30 *King Eyambo's Palace, Calabar River, Africa. Prefabricated by John Walker in London, 1843–44.*

XV 31 *Palm Stove, Royal Botanic Gardens, Kew. By Decimus Burton and Richard Turner, 1845–47. Exterior.*

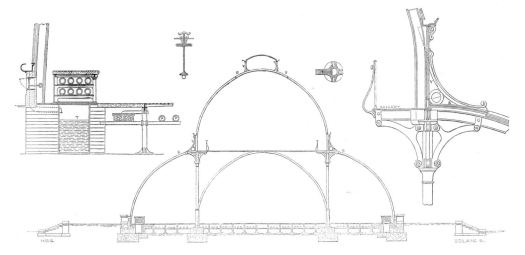

XV 32 and 33 *Palm Stove, Kew. Interior, section, and details.*

XV 34   Britannia Bridge, Menai Strait, Wales. By Robert Stephenson and Francis Thompson, 1845–50. (The Menai Bridge in the distance is by Thomas Telford, 1819–24.)

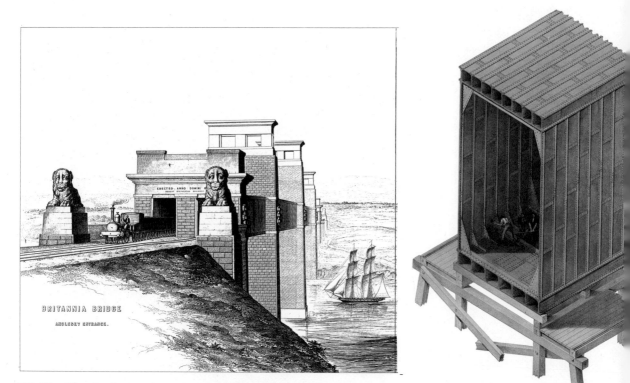

XV 35   The Anglesey entrance, with lions by John Thomas.

XV 36   Section of tube.

XV 37 *Tubular Bridge, Conway, Wales. By Robert Stephenson and Francis Thompson, 1845–49.*
Floating the second tube into position to be hoisted.

XV 38 *Britannia Bridge. Details of central pier.*

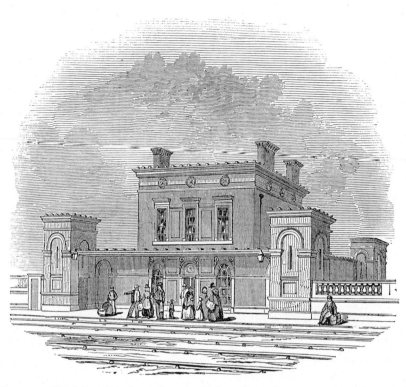

XV 39   *Chester and Holyhead Railway Station, Holywell, Wales. By Francis Thompson, 1847–48.*

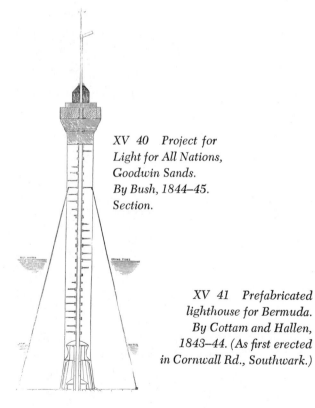

XV 40   *Project for Light for All Nations, Goodwin Sands. By Bush, 1844–45. Section.*

XV 41   *Prefabricated lighthouse for Bermuda. By Cottam and Hallen, 1843–44. (As first erected in Cornwall Rd., Southwark.)*

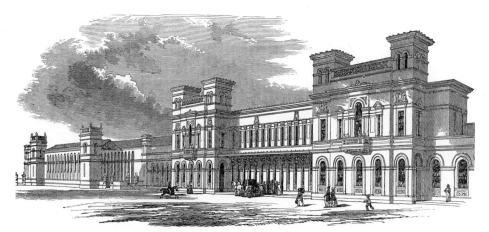

XV 42   General Station, Chester. By Robert Stephenson and Francis Thompson, 1844–48.

XV 43   General Station, Chester. Sheds.

XV 44   Paragon Railway Station Hotel, Hull. By T. G. Andrews, 1847–48. Queen Victoria arriving.

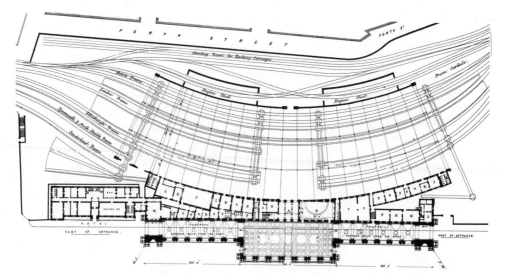

XV 45 *Central Station, Newcastle-on-Tyne. By John Dobson, 1846–50. Plan.*

XV 46 *Central Station, Newcastle-on-Tyne. The sheds.*

XV 47 *Shoreditch II Railway Station, London. By Sancton Wood, 1848–49. The sheds.*

XV 48   Sailors' Home, Canning Pl., Liverpool.
By John Cunningham, 1846–49. Section showing cast-iron galleries in court.

XV 49   Euston II Railway Station, London.
By P. C. Hardwick, 1846–49. Great Hall.

XV 50   Sailors' Home, Liverpool.
Entrance gates.

XV 51   Prefabricated buildings
awaiting shipment at Samuel Hemming's Clift-House Iron Building Works near Bristol in 1854.

XV 53   Prefabricated iron warehouse, with living rooms
above, for export to San Francisco. By E. T. Bellhouse, 1850.

XV 52   Prefabricated iron and glazed
terra cotta clock tower for Geelong,
Australia. By James Edmeston, 1854.

XV 54   Prefabricated iron ballroom, Balmoral Castle,
near Ballater, Fifeshire. By E. T. Bellhouse, 1851.

XVI THE CRYSTAL PALACE:

FERRO-VITREOUS TRIUMPH

AND ENSUING REACTION

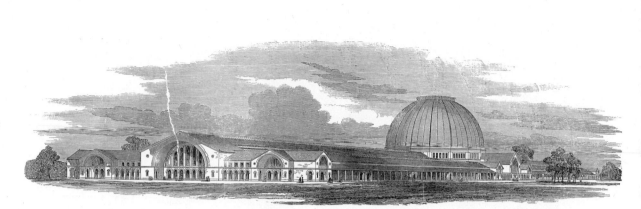

XVI 1   *Official Design for the Edifice for the Great Exhibition of 1851. By Building Committee of Royal Commission, 1850. From* Illustrated London News, *22 June 1850.*

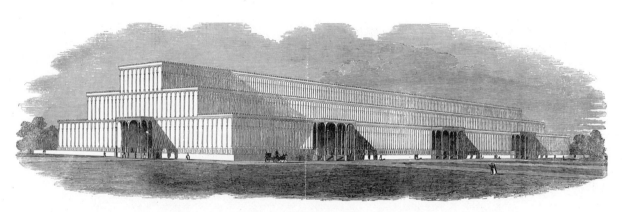

XVI 2   *First developed design for Crystal Palace I. By Sir Joseph Paxton, June 1850. As published in* Illustrated London News, *6 July 1850.*

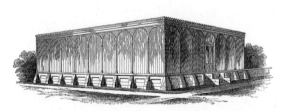
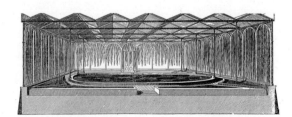

XVI 3   *Lily House, Chatsworth, Derbyshire. By Sir Joseph Paxton, 1849–50. Perspective and section.*

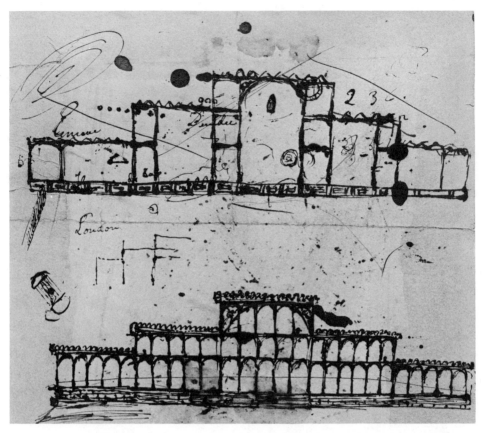

XVI 4 *Original sketch for Crystal Palace. By Sir Joseph Paxton, middle of June 1850.*

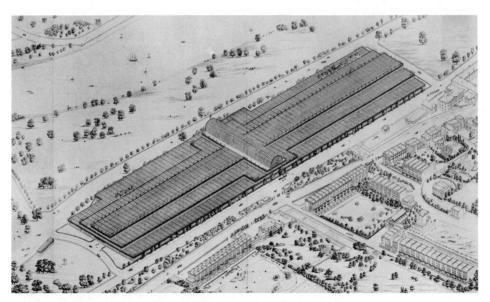

XVI 5 *Crystal Palace I, Hyde Park, London.*
By Sir Joseph Paxton, and Fox and Henderson, 1 August 1850–1 May 1851. Birdseye view.

XVI 6   *Crystal Palace, Hyde Park,*
London. By Sir Joseph Paxton, and Fox and Henderson, 1850–51. End view.

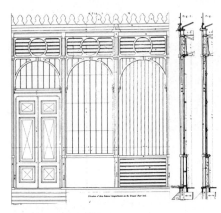

XVI 7   *Standard*
bay elevation.

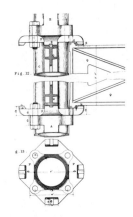

XVI 8   *Details of*
stanchions and girders.

XVI 9   *Looking across the nave at gallery level.*

XVI 10   *Midland Station, Park End St., Oxford. By Fox and Henderson, 1851–52. Entrance porch and sheds.*

XVI 11   Sash-bar machine used at site during erection of Crystal Palace I, Hyde Park, London.

XVI 12   Early stage in construction of Crystal Palace I. October 1850.

XVI 13   *Preparation of sub-assemblies at site for Crystal Palace I. November 1850.*

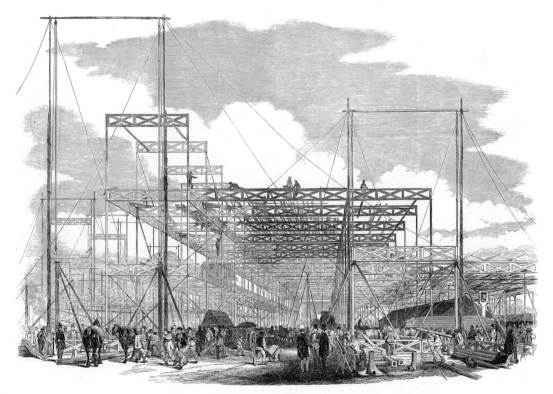

XVI 14   *Crystal Palace I in construction. November 1850.*

XVI 15   *Crystal Palace I, Hyde Park, London. By Sir Joseph Paxton, and Fox and Henderson, 1 August 1850–1 May 1851. Transept with Sibthorp Elm.*

XVI 16   *Nave before installation of exhibits. January 1851.*

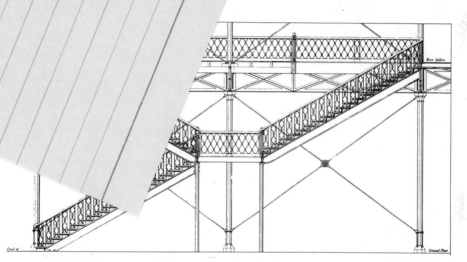

...hange, London. By Sir Joseph Paxton, 1851.

XVI 18   Detailing of railings in Crystal Palace I. By Owen Jones, 1850–51.

XVI 19   Project for New York Crystal Palace. By Sir Joseph Paxton, 1852.

XVI 20   Project for reconstruction of Crystal Palace at Sydenham. By Sir Joseph Paxton, 1852.

XVI 21   Project for Exercise-Room,
London Hospital for Diseases of the Chest, Victoria Park, London. By Sir Joseph Paxton, 1851.

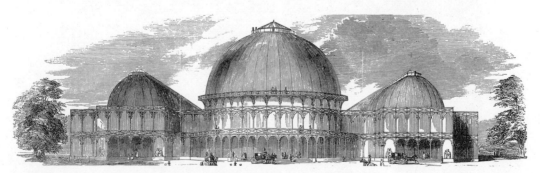

XVI 22   Crystal Palace, Dublin. By Sir John Benson, 1852–53. Exterior.

XVI 23 *Crystal Palace, Dublin. Interior.*

XVI 24   Crystal Palace II, Sydenham. By Sir Joseph Paxton,
and Fox, Henderson and Co., 1852–54. Exterior.

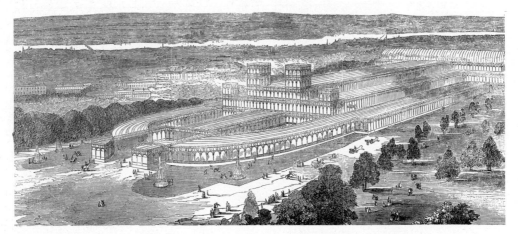

XVI 25   Project for extending Crystal Palace I. By Sir Joseph Paxton, 1852.

XVI 26   *Crystal Palace II, Sydenham. By Sir Joseph Paxton, and Fox, Henderson and Co., 1852–54. Interior.*

XVI 27   *Lord Warden Railway Hotel, Dover. By Samuel Beazley, 1850–53.*

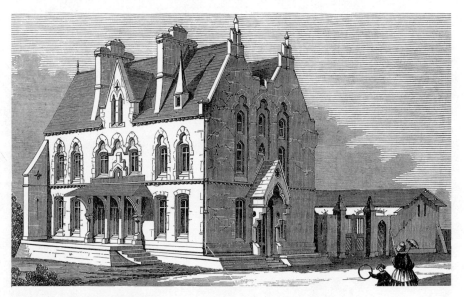

XVI 28   *Southerndown Hotel, near Bridgend, Glamorganshire.*
By J. P. Seddon, 1852–53.

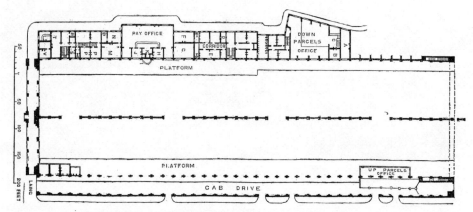

XVI 29   *Great Northern Railway Station, King's Cross, London.*
By Lewis Cubitt, (1850) 1851–52. Plan.

XVI 30 *King's Cross Railway Station, London. By Lewis Cubitt,
(1850) 1851–52. Front of sheds on day of opening, 14 October 1852.*

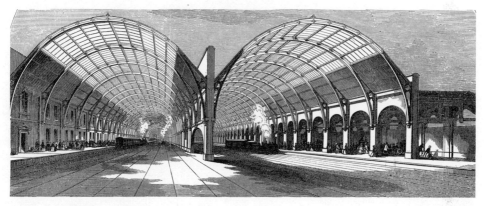

XVI 31 *Section of sheds.*

XVI 32 *Front of sheds today.*

XVI 33 *King's Cross Railway Station,*
London. By Lewis Cubitt,
(1850) 1851–52.
Laminated wooden arched
trusses and cast-iron shoes.

XVI 34 *Paddington II*
Railway Station, London.
By I. K. Brunel and M. D. Wyatt,
1852–54. One of "transepts"
connecting the three sheds.

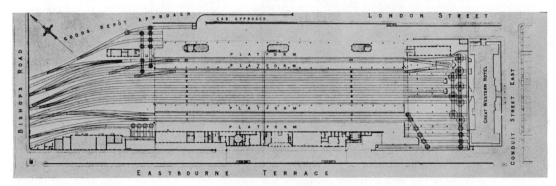

XVI 35 *Paddington II Railway Station, London. Original plan.*

XVI 36   Paddington II. Sheds.

XVI 37   Paddington II. Interior wall of station block.

XVI 38 *"The Railway Station." By William P. Frith, 1861.*

XVI 39 *Paddington II. Stationmaster's oriel.*

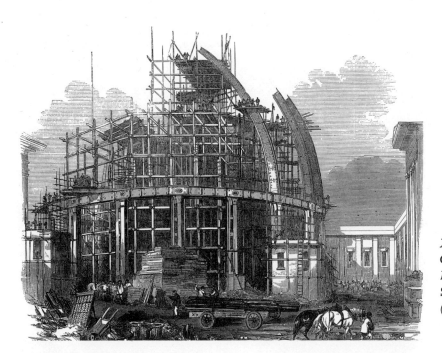

XVI 40 *British Museum, Great Russell St., London. Reading Room by Sydney Smirke in construction (1852) 1854–57.*

XVI 41 *Reading Room. Interior.*

XVI 42 *"The Aerial Ballet
of the Brompton Boilermakers."
(The Museum of Science
and Art, Brompton Park,
London, by Young and Son,
in construction, 1855–56.)*

XVI 43 *Museum of Science
and Art. Sidewalls in construction.*

XVI 44 *Museum of Science
and Art. Roof in construction.*

XVI 45   *Museum of Science and Art. Galleries before completion.*

XVI 46   *Interior at official opening.*

XVI 47 *Museum of Science and Art, London. By Young and Son, 1855–56. Entrance porch.*

XVII RUSKIN OR BUTTERFIELD?

VICTORIAN GOTHIC AT THE MID-CENTURY

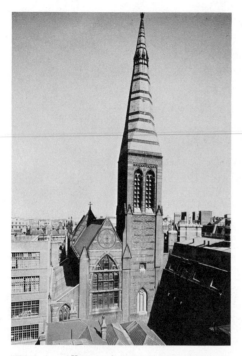

XVII 1 *All Saints', Margaret St., Regent St., London. William Butterfield, (1849) 1850–(1852)–1859. West front and tower.*

XVII 2 *First published view of exterior, January 1853.*

XVII 3 *South buttress with "Annunciation" relief.*

XVII 4 *Juxtaposition of south porch, tower shaft, and choir school.*

XVII 5   *All Saints', Margaret St., London. Interior.*

*XVII 6 All Saints', Margaret St., London.
Nave arcade and chancel arch.*

XVII 7 South aisle.

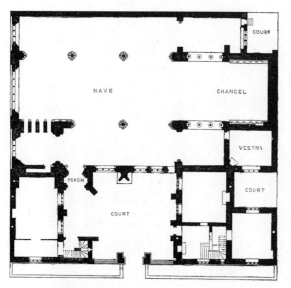

XVII 8 Plan.

XVII 9 Interior looking east.

XVII 10 *Choir School and Clergy House of All Saints', Margaret St.*

XVII 11 *All Saints', Margaret St. North wall of chancel.*

XVII 12 *St. Thomas's, Leeds. By William Butterfield, 1850–52.*

XVII 13   Original project for St. Matthias's,
Stoke Newington, London.
By William Butterfield, 1850.

XVII 14   St. Matthias's, Howard Rd.,Stoke
Newington, London. By William Butterfield,
(1850) 1851–53. The east end after blitz.

XVII 15   West front after blitz.